My Story, My Art.
La Mia Storia, La Mia Arte.

Autobiography of a forgotten 1940s Italian Surrealist

By Antonia Pageta, Anthony D Padgett & Ghost (In The Machine) Writer

Published by

Ghost In The Machine Writer

First Published 2023

CHAPTER 1

My earliest memory is of a warm summer evening when I, Antonia Pageta, opened my eyes to my destiny. The sun had begun to set in our quaint Italian village, casting a golden hue against the terracotta walls of the small room where my mother, Silvia, cradled me in her arms. She looked down at me with wonder and love, her eyes filled with an indescribable joy.

"Antonia," she whispered, as if saying my name out loud would somehow make this moment even more real. "My beautiful little girl."

I didn't understand much about the world. Still, something deep within me knew that my life would be anything but ordinary. There was a sense of destiny hanging in the air, like the scent of fresh paint on a canvas waiting for the first brushstroke.

The room was small, yet filled with warmth and comfort. My mother had carefully created a space that radiated love and security. The walls were adorned with hand-painted murals of delicate flowers and intricate patterns, each stroke lovingly applied by Silvia herself. As I would later learn, my mother possessed a natural talent for art that she would pass on to me.

"Look at her, Silvia," came a voice from the doorway. It was my father, Maurizio, standing there with a mixture of pride and awe on his face. "She's perfect."

"Isn't she?" Silvia replied, her voice brimming with happiness. "I can already see the artist in her, Maurizio. Just look at those tiny hands – they'll create such beautiful works one day."

The atmosphere in the room was electrifying, as if joy and excitement had infused every fiber of the space. I could feel the energy pulsating around me, wrapping me up in its warm embrace. I was surrounded by love, and in that moment, I knew that I was destined for greatness.

"Antonia," my mother whispered again, her eyes never leaving mine. "You are going to do incredible things, my sweet girl. I can feel it."

I couldn't comprehend the full weight of her words, but somehow, I understood their significance. The passion for art that had been passed down through generations of my family was now coursing through my veins, ready to shape me into the artist I would become. And though I had only just begun my journey, the fire within me burned brightly, fueled by the love and support of my beloved mother, Silvia.

As I lay there in my mother's arms, the door to the small room creaked further open, and in walked my father, Maurizio Pageta. He was a tall man with broad shoulders and dark, serious eyes that seemed to hold the weight of the world. He took slow, measured steps towards us, his gaze locking onto me as if trying to decipher some hidden message.

"Isn't she beautiful, Maurizio?" Silvia asked, beaming at him with maternal pride. "Our little Antonia."

"Si," he murmured, his voice rough with emotion. "She is a gift."

My mother smiled warmly, her love for my father evident in every line of her face. But there was something else behind her eyes - a flicker of defiance, perhaps, or the unspoken knowledge that their dreams for me were not perfectly aligned.

"Look at her hands, Maurizio," Silvia repeated, gently lifting one of my tiny fists into view. "I believe she will be an extraordinary artist someday."

4

"An artist?" My father's eyebrows furrowed as he considered this possibility. "Silvia, you know how difficult it can be for women to succeed in that profession. Besides, we need her to help with the family business when she grows up."

"Times are changing, Maurizio," Silvia insisted, passion rising in her voice. "Our daughter has a talent that cannot be denied or suppressed. We must nurture it, help it grow."

My father sighed heavily, rubbing his brow with a calloused hand. "I want what's best for her too, Silvia. But we must be practical. Art may not put food on the table."

"Can we not give her the chance to choose her own path?" my mother pleaded, her eyes welling up with tears. "If she has a gift for art, shouldn't we support her in pursuing it?"

"Silvia, I..." Maurizio hesitated, torn between his love for me and his desire to protect me from a world that might not appreciate my talents.

As I lay there in my mother's arms, I could feel the tension building between them. It was as if the very air in the room had become charged with their conflicting desires, filling the space with an electric current that seemed to vibrate against my skin. Though I didn't understand the specifics of their conversation, I could sense the importance of this moment - the first of many battles that would be fought over my future.

"Fine," my father relented, his expression softening as he looked at Silvia. "We will encourage her passion for art, but we must also teach her the value of hard work and responsibility."

"Agreed," my mother whispered, her eyes shining with gratitude. "Together, we'll give Antonia the best life we possibly can."

And so, in that small, dimly lit room, my parents made a pact that would shape the course of my life. They vowed to support me, to guide me, and to help me navigate the turbulent waters that lay ahead. But even as they made these promises, the seeds of conflict had been sown - seeds that would grow into towering trees, casting long shadows over our lives and testing the bonds of family.

I may have been just a small girl, but somehow, I understood that my journey would not be an easy one. And yet, with the love of my mother and the strength of my father behind me, I felt ready to face whatever challenges awaited me.

The warmth of my mother's arms enveloped me as I nestled against her chest. The room around us was alive with the scents of fresh bread and fragrant herbs - the earthy aroma of rosemary mingling with the sweet perfume of basil and thyme. Flickering candlelight danced across the rough-hewn walls, casting shadows that seemed to sway in time with my mother's gentle rocking.

"Look at her, Maurizio," Silvia cooed, her voice thick with emotion. "Our daughter is so beautiful. I can see the light of creativity shining in her eyes."

My father stood by the window, his brow furrowed as he stared out into the night. The wind whispered through the trees outside, their leaves rustling like a thousand tiny hushed voices. He turned to look at us, his face softened by the glow of the candles.

"I know, Silvia," he said, his voice heavy with concern. "But I worry for her future. Our village is not kind to those who dream too big or reach too high."

My mother shifted me gently in her arms, her eyes never leaving my face. "We will teach her to be strong, Maurizio. We'll guide her path and help her find her way in this world."

"Strength alone may not be enough," my father replied, his hands clenching into fists at his sides. "The world can be cruel, especially to those who dare to defy tradition."

"Then we must show it that some traditions are meant to be broken," my mother declared, a fire igniting in her eyes. "That our Antonia has a gift, and it should not be stifled."

I could feel the tension between my parents, like a taut rope straining to hold two opposing forces together. Their voices were calm, but underneath the surface, I sensed a battle raging - a struggle between my father's desire for stability and my mother's belief in the power of art.

"Silvia," my father said, his voice cracking with emotion. "I want our daughter to be happy, to live a life free of hardship. But I also want her to understand the importance of family, of tradition. She must learn to balance her dreams with her roots."

"Then we will teach her both," my mother replied, determination in her voice. "We'll show her that love is stronger than any obstacle, and that she can forge her own path without losing sight of where she came from."

And so, as I lay there in my mother's arms, surrounded by the heady scents of herbs and the tender lullaby of rustling leaves, I felt the weight of their hopes and fears for my future. Even then, I knew that I would need to find a way to reconcile my passion for art with my father's traditional views, to prove that one could coexist with the other.

In that moment, I vowed to myself that I would not let them down. I would embrace both the light and the shadows of my heritage, using them as fuel to create a life that was uniquely mine. And though the road ahead would be filled with challenges and heartache, I was determined to face it all, head held high, with the strength of my parents by my side.

With my tiny hands, I reached out and grasped a nearby charcoal stick that my mother had been using to sketch the picturesque scenery outside our window. At just a few years old, I could not yet comprehend the significance of this simple act or the potential it held.

"Look at her, Maurizio," Silvia whispered excitedly, as I smeared the charcoal onto the rough wooden floorboards. "She already has an artist's touch."

My father, leaning against the doorframe with his arms folded, frowned and shook his head. "It's just a child's curiosity, Silvia. Don't put such ideas in her head."

"Can't you see it, though?" my mother insisted, eyes shining with pride and joy. "Our Antonia has something special about her. There is a fire in her eyes, a determination that cannot be denied."

"Silvia, all children are curious," my father replied, his voice weary but gentle. "I don't want her to grow up believing she has no other choice but to chase after such frivolous dreams. It's our duty to prepare her for the real world, not some fantasy."

As my parents spoke, their words washing over me like waves upon a shore, I felt a spark ignite within my infant heart. Though I was still too young to fully understand the complexities of their conversation, I sensed the power of my actions and the impact they had on those around me.

"Her passion is not frivolous, Maurizio," my mother said, her face set in an expression of fierce determination. "If we nurture her talent, if we give her the freedom to explore, who knows what wonders she might create?"

"Art won't feed her, Silvia," my father argued, his concern evident in the furrow between his brows. "Nor will it shelter her from the harsh realities of life. We must teach her practical skills, show her the value of hard work and dedication."

"Art can be both beautiful and practical," my mother countered. "It can open doors, create opportunities, and inspire others. We should not stifle her potential out of fear."

Though I couldn't yet comprehend the weight of their words, my instincts urged me to continue reaching for that charcoal, to keep making marks on the floor. I felt an inexplicable connection to this simple act of creation, a sense of purpose that would only grow stronger as I experienced the world around me.

As I continued to scribble my infantile masterpiece, my parents' voices faded into the background, their debate continuing long into the night. But even then, in those earliest days of my life, I knew that art was more than just a fleeting desire or childish whim. It was a calling that echoed through my very being, a passion that would shape not only my future but also the lives of those who crossed my path.

And so, with every stroke of charcoal against wood, I began to carve out a destiny that defied expectations and transcended the limitations imposed upon me. My journey had only just begun, and already I could feel the winds of change stirring in the air, carrying me forward to a life filled with beauty, color, and the unwavering belief in the power of one's dreams.

The cold, unforgiving wind whipped through the narrow Italian streets, but as I walked alongside Giovanni, my oldest friend and fellow artist, my heart felt warm with anticipation. We were on our way to an art exhibition, a chance to showcase my latest works that had consumed me for months. The emotions of my childhood still lingered within me, further fueling my passion for creating art.

"Antonia, your pieces will be incredible tonight," Giovanni reassured me, his voice steady and encouraging. "I've seen your progress over the years, and you've truly outdone yourself."

"Thank you, Giovanni," I said, appreciating the support he'd always given me. "But there's still so much more to do, to prove myself in this world."

"Your father may never understand, but it doesn't mean you should give up on your dreams." He looked at me, concern etching itself across his face.

"Si, I know," I sighed, recalling the countless arguments with my father over the years. Despite his resistance, I was grateful for my mother's unwavering belief in my abilities — she had always been my rock and guiding light.

As we entered the gallery, the scent of fresh paint and varnish filled my nostrils. The polished wooden floors gleamed beneath the soft lighting, and the sound of hushed conversations surrounded us. My heart raced with a mix of excitement and apprehension, my palms damp with nerves.

"Signorina Pageta, your artwork is truly captivating," Enzo Romano, a dashing fashion photographer, approached me with a charming smile. "I've never seen such a unique perspective before."

"Thank you, Signor Romano," I replied, trying to hide my rising blush. His flattery was intoxicating, but I couldn't lose sight of my true purpose — my art. It was a constant battle within me, to be seen for my work and not just my beauty.

"Antonia, I wanted to introduce you to Lucia Moretti," Giovanni said, pulling me away from Enzo's magnetic presence. "She's an activist fighting for justice and equality."

"Buonasera, Lucia," I greeted her warmly, sensing a kindred spirit in her fiery eyes.

"Your art speaks volumes, Antonia," Lucia said with admiration. "It's inspiring to see a woman like you pushing boundaries and challenging the status quo."

As the evening unfolded, a sense of pride swelled within me. My artwork captured the attention of many, but I couldn't help but feel the ghost of my father's disapproval lingering in the shadows. It was a constant reminder of my need to prove myself, to forge my own path despite the expectations placed upon me.

My thoughts raced as I observed those who admired my paintings, their eyes fixed on the vibrant colors and surreal imagery. Would my father ever accept my passion? Or would I always be caught between my love for art and my desire for his approval?

Only time would tell, but one thing was certain: my journey had only just begun, and I was determined to make my mark on the world — no matter the obstacles that stood in my way.

CHAPTER 2

I still remember the day I met Giovanni Bellini. We were just children, both of us with wide, curious eyes and an insatiable hunger for color and expression. It was a warm summer day in our small Italian village, and the sun painted everything golden as it began to set.

"Antonia," he had called out to me, his voice barely above a whisper as he approached. "Do you want to draw with me? I saw your painting in the school exhibition, and it was amazing."

"Really?" I blinked up at him, my heart fluttering like a caged bird in my chest. No one had ever complimented my art before, let alone wanted to create alongside me. I nodded eagerly, a smile spreading across my face. "I'd love to, Giovanni."

And so, our shared passion for art began. Day after day, we would steal away to the quiet corners of our village where the world seemed to slow down just for us. We would spread out our sketchbooks, pencils, and brushes, and lose ourselves in the magic of creation. Our laughter would mingle with the hum of cicadas and the soft rustling of leaves overhead as we brought our visions to life on paper and canvas.

"Look at this," Giovanni would say, holding up his latest work – a delicate landscape with the tiniest hint of a castle hidden among the trees. His hands, which were always covered in paint, trembled with excitement. He would wait for my response, his brown eyes searching mine for approval.

"Wow, that's incredible!" I'd exclaim, genuinely amazed by his talent. "How did you get the colors to blend so smoothly?"

Giovanni would then lean over my shoulder, pointing out the techniques he used while I soaked in every word, eager to learn from my dear friend. In return, I would show him my own paintings, my surrealist visions of worlds that existed only in my dreams.

"Antonia, this is so unique," he'd say, his voice filled with admiration. "I could never think of something like this."

"Maybe you can," I'd reply, a mischievous glint in my eyes. "You just need to let your imagination run wild."

As we continued to draw and paint together, our bond only grew stronger. The hours we spent side by side, sharing our thoughts and dreams, became some of the most cherished memories of my childhood. It was as if Giovanni and I spoke a secret language – one made up of brushstrokes and charcoal lines that wove an invisible thread between us.

"Promise me something, Antonia," he said to me one warm afternoon as we sat beneath the shade of an ancient oak tree, our latest creations drying in the sun. "Promise me that no matter where life takes us, we'll always have art. We'll always have each other."

"Of course," I replied without hesitation, my heart swelling with affection for my best friend. "I promise, Giovanni." And with those words, we sealed our pact, two young souls bound together by the shared passion that would shape our lives forever.

Over the years, our friendship grew like the wildflowers that adorned the hillsides of our small village. The seeds of creativity and shared passion blossomed into a vibrant, colorful garden of trust and support. Giovanni and I became more than just friends; we were each other's confidantes, muses, and critics.

"Antonia, try adding some cerulean blue to the sky," Giovanni suggested one day as we painted in the fields, the sun casting its golden rays upon us. "It'll give it more depth."

"Great idea," I replied, dipping my brush into the paint and gliding it across the canvas. "And for your landscape, maybe use a touch of yellow ochre for the highlights in the grass."

We pushed each other to explore new techniques and ideas, our imaginations soaring higher with each stroke of the brush. Our days were spent in a whirlwind of creation, and our nights were filled with dreams of the masterpieces we'd someday paint.

One day, as Giovanni and I worked on a particularly challenging piece, my mother, Silvia, came to check on us. She had always been my rock – loving, supportive, and wise beyond her years.

"Antonia, carissima, your work is coming along beautifully," she said, smiling warmly at me as she examined my latest painting. Her eyes sparkled with pride and love.

"Thank you, Mamma," I replied, beaming back at her. "Giovanni helped me with the composition."

"Ah, Giovanni, you are becoming quite an artist yourself," she praised him, placing a gentle hand on his shoulder. "You both have such talent. It brings me joy to see you pursue your dreams together."

Silvia's unwavering support nurtured not only my talents but also the bond between Giovanni and me. Over homemade pasta dinners, she would listen intently as we excitedly recounted our latest artistic discoveries and victories. She became a beacon of encouragement and wisdom, guiding us along the winding path towards our dreams.

"Remember, Antonia," she once told me as we sat by the fire one evening, "your passion for art is a gift. Don't let anyone ever convince you otherwise. Keep creating, keep dreaming, and let your heart guide you."

Her words were like warm embers, igniting my determination to never give up on my dreams – no matter the challenges that lay ahead. And with Giovanni by my side, those challenges seemed surmountable.

"Thank you, Mamma," I whispered, tears welling in my eyes. "I promise, I'll always create. I'll always dream."

"Brava, Antonia," she said softly, pulling me into a tender embrace. "And remember, you and Giovanni will always have each other."

That night, as I drifted off to sleep, I knew that our friendship was more than just a shared love for art. It was an unbreakable bond, forged by creativity, passion, and the unwavering support of those who believed in us. And as long as we had each other, there was nothing we couldn't accomplish.

A cacophony of clattering dishes and swift footsteps filled the air as my father, Maurizio, bustled about our small kitchen. I could tell by the furrowed brow that he wore like a badge of honor that something was weighing on his mind. As my mother, Silvia, set the table for dinner, she cast me a knowing glance, signaling that it was time for another conversation.

"Antonia," Papa began hesitantly, "your mother and I have been talking, and we are concerned about how much time you are spending with Giovanni."

My heart sank, but I braced myself for the familiar argument. "Papa, Giovanni is my best friend, and we both love art. What's wrong with that?"

"Art is all well and good, Antonia, but you are young, and the world can be a dangerous place," he replied, his voice wavering between concern and frustration. "You know I only want what is best for you, my dear."

"Your father is right, Antonia," Mamma interjected gently. "It's just that his way of showing his love might not always align with your dreams."

I knew they both loved me, but it was difficult to see past the cloud of doubt and skepticism that hung over my father's words. Still, I couldn't let his fears dictate my life or my friendship with Giovanni.

"Thank you for your concern, Papa, but I trust Giovanni, and I believe in our passion for art," I proclaimed, my voice steady and resolute. "We will help each other grow as artists, and we won't let anything stand in our way."

"Antonia, I don't doubt your intentions, but please understand that I worry for your safety and future," Papa pleaded, his eyes softening. "Promise me you'll be careful."

"Of course, Papa," I assured him, my gaze unwavering. "I promise I'll be careful."

The following morning, as Giovanni and I sat beneath our favorite tree, sketchbooks in hand, we spoke about the conversation with my parents. I expressed my fears and frustrations, and Giovanni listened intently, his eyes filled with empathy and understanding.

"Antonia, your father's concerns come from a place of love," he reassured me. "But we can't let fear hold us back. We have to keep pushing ourselves, honing our craft, and supporting each other."

"Exactly," I agreed, my determination surging like a tidal wave. "We won't let anything stand in our way, Giovanni. Not even Papa's skepticism."

"Never," Giovanni affirmed, his voice filled with conviction. "No matter what, our friendship and artistic pursuits will always come first."

As we continued to sketch and paint under the dappled sunlight, our bond grew stronger with each brushstroke.

Despite the shadow of doubt cast by my father, we remained steadfast in our shared passion for art and our unwavering support for one another.

"Thank you, Giovanni," I whispered, gratitude swelling in my chest. "For everything."

"Always, Antonia," he replied, his eyes shining with warmth. "Together, we'll defy the odds and create something truly extraordinary."

The sun dipped low in the sky, casting a golden glow on the lush, rolling hills of the Italian countryside. I sat beside Giovanni, my sketchbook propped up against my knees as we both worked feverishly to capture the scene before us. The rustling leaves and distant birdsong provided a serene soundtrack to our artistic endeavors.

"Antonia, look at this," Giovanni said, tilting his sketchbook so I could see his work. His rendering of the landscape was exquisite, with every delicate detail carefully captured. "What do you think?"

"Wow, Giovanni," I breathed, genuinely impressed. "Your attention to detail is incredible. Teach me how you do it?"

"Of course," he grinned, moving closer to guide my hand as I attempted to mimic his technique. "You just need to pay close attention to the smallest elements; they all come together to create the larger picture."

As we continued working side by side, we challenged each other, sharing tips and tricks to improve our skills. We experimented with different mediums, from charcoal to watercolors, pushing ourselves to refine our techniques and grow as artists. Our shared love for art fueled our desire to become better, and our friendship only grew stronger in the process.

It wasn't just our artistic pursuits that bonded us; we relied on one another to navigate the complexities of adolescence.

When my grandmother passed away, Giovanni was there to offer a shoulder to cry on. He held my hand through the funeral and whispered words of comfort as I grieved. In turn, when his family faced financial struggles, I did everything I could to support him emotionally. We were there for one another, no matter what life threw our way.

"Antonia, I don't know what I would've done without you during these tough times," Giovanni confessed one evening as we sat beneath our favorite tree, the sunset painting the sky in brilliant hues.

"Neither do I, Giovanni," I admitted, my voice thick with emotion. "Your friendship means everything to me."

"Likewise," he said softly, squeezing my hand in reassurance. "Together, we'll face whatever life has in store for us."

Our shared experiences and unwavering support for one another carried us through all the joys and heartaches of growing up. Our love for art and our dedication to improving our skills went hand in hand with the emotional connection that bound us together. In each other, we found not only an artistic companion but also a true friend who would stand by our side through thick and thin.

The sound of laughter echoed through the warm Italian summer air as we sat under the shade of our favorite tree, paintbrushes in hand. Giovanni and I had spent countless hours there, pouring our hearts onto the canvas, allowing our imaginations to take flight.

"Remember that time we painted the entire side of your father's barn with a mural of fantastical creatures?" Giovanni grinned, his eyes sparkling with mischief and nostalgia.

I laughed heartily at the memory. "Oh, how could I forget? My father was so furious! But, after seeing how much joy it brought to the villagers, he couldn't stay mad for long."

"Ah, yes," Giovanni mused, dipping his brush into a vibrant shade of blue. "We were just children then, but even then, our passion for art was evident."

Our friendship had been the fertile soil from which our artistic talents had grown and blossomed. We challenged each other's perspectives, pushing one another to explore new techniques and styles. Our bond was the foundation upon which our passions were built, the inspiration that led us both to pursue a life dedicated to creativity.

"Antonia, remember when we snuck into the church late at night to study the frescoes?" he asked, my voice filled with warmth and fondness.

"Of course," I replied, my eyes lighting up at the memory. "We spent hours analyzing every detail, trying to understand the artist's intentions and technique. It was magical."

"Indeed, it was," Giovanni agreed, the corners of his mouth turning upwards in a contented smile. "That night, I truly understood the power of art—to transcend time and space, to connect people across generations."

As we continued painting, our conversation drifted to other cherished memories: the time we staged an impromptu art exhibition in the village square, drawing a curious crowd of onlookers; the day we painted portraits of one another, capturing each other's essence on canvas with loving precision; the countless sunsets we spent together, our hearts soaring with the boundless possibilities of the future.

"Antonia," Giovanni said softly, gazing at me with a mixture of admiration and affection. "I want you to know that I am eternally grateful for your friendship. You've inspired me in ways I could never have imagined."

Tears welled up in my eyes as I looked back at him. "Giovanni, without you, I would never have found the courage to follow my dreams. You've been my rock, my muse, and my dearest friend."

We fell silent, allowing the weight of our words to settle between us. Our connection, borne from a shared love of art and a lifetime of memories, was a testament to the indelible impact we had on each other's lives. Together, we had shaped each other into the artists we were destined to become, forever entwined by the threads of our passion and the warmth of our friendship.

The sun was setting, casting a warm golden glow across the small studio where Giovanni and I sat, our easels side by side. The scent of oil paint and turpentine mingled with the aroma of freshly brewed coffee, creating an intoxicating blend that never failed to transport me back to our childhood days.

"Remember that summer when we painted landscapes in the fields?" Giovanni asked, his brush dancing across the canvas as he added delicate strokes of color.

I smiled, recalling the vibrant hues of wildflowers and the endless expanse of azure sky. "We spent every day outside, trying to capture the beauty of nature. We were so young and full of dreams."

"Indeed," he replied, his eyes meeting mine for a moment before returning to his work. "And now, look at us; still chasing those dreams, side by side."

There was something comforting in the familiarity of it all, the rhythm of our brushes and the shared silence between us, punctuated only by the occasional words of encouragement or admiration for each other's work.

"Antonia," Giovanni said suddenly, a seriousness entering his tone. "Do you ever wonder where we'd be without each other?"

I paused, my brush hovering above the palette as I considered his question. "Honestly, Giovanni, I can't imagine my life without you by my side. We've grown together, learned from each other, and pushed one another to become the artists we are today."

He nodded solemnly. "Our friendship has been a constant source of inspiration and support. I don't think either of us would have gotten this far without the other."

As I dipped my brush into a pool of cerulean blue, I couldn't help but agree. Our journey had been a winding one, filled with triumphs and setbacks, but through it all, our bond had remained unshakable.

"Even now," I mused aloud, "our friendship continues to shape our work. I see your influence in every stroke of my brush, and I hope you can see mine in yours."

"Always," he replied, his voice filled with warmth.

A sense of gratitude washed over me as I looked at Giovanni, his brow furrowed in concentration as he worked on his latest masterpiece. Our friendship had been the foundation upon which we'd built our lives, a powerful connection that had carried us through the years and into the present.

As the sun dipped below the horizon, casting our studio in a soft, golden light, I knew that no matter where our artistic paths took us, we would remain bound by our shared passion, our unwavering determination, and most importantly, our enduring love for one another.

CHAPTER 3

I stood at the entrance of the prestigious Accademia delle Belle Arti, my heart pounding with a mixture of excitement and trepidation. As a young woman with an insatiable passion for art, I knew that pursuing it as a career was my destiny. The male-dominated world did not deter me; instead, it fueled my determination. My name is Antonia Pageta, and I was born to be an artist.

"Signorina Pageta," Professor Marino greeted me warmly as I entered the hallowed halls of the academy, "welcome to your first day." His eyes scanned me up and down, assessing my potential. He was a tall, stoic man with a reputation for being one of the best instructors in the school.

"Thank you, Professor," I replied, trying to keep my voice steady. "I'm honored to be here."

The academy itself was a masterpiece – centuries-old frescoes adorned the walls, and the smell of oil paint and turpentine lingered in the air. Strolling through its corridors felt like walking through history, surrounded by the spirits of the great artists who once graced these halls.

During each class, I soaked up every word my professors uttered, as if their wisdom could provide me with the key to unlocking my full potential. I listened intently to their critiques and suggestions, eager to grow and improve. Despite my gender and the whispers that followed me from classroom to classroom, I refused to let anything hold me back.

"Miss Pageta," Professor Marino addressed me one day while examining my latest creation. His usually stern face softened as he studied the piece, his eyebrows raised in appreciation. "You have a unique talent, and your dedication is evident."

"Thank you, Professor," I said, blushing but filled with pride. "I've been inspired by the Surrealists, and I try to incorporate their ideas into my work."

"Ah, yes," he nodded thoughtfully. "I can see the influence of Dalí and Magritte in this piece." He gestured to the canvas, where a distorted clock melted over a barren tree, while a lonely apple floated just out of reach.

"Keep pushing yourself, Antonia," he continued. "You have the potential to leave a lasting mark on the art world."

As I delved deeper into my studies at the art school, I found myself immersed in a world of boundless creativity and endless possibilities. Every day, I pushed myself to explore new techniques, styles, and ideas, driven by my passion for Surrealism and its ability to defy reality.

"Antonia, come here," called Professor Marino from across the studio. I walked over, clutching my paintbrushes and palette, eager to understand his perspective on my work.

"Look at this," he said, directing my gaze to the painting before us. The canvas featured an ethereal landscape, with a floating city suspended in the sky and a waterfall cascading into the abyss below. "Your use of color and composition is captivating. But tell me, what inspired this particular piece?"

"Thank you, Professor," I replied, my heart swelling with pride. "The dreamlike quality of Surrealist paintings has always resonated with me. This piece, specifically, was influenced by the works of Yves Tanguy and Max Ernst."

"Ah, I see," he nodded, his eyes scanning every detail of the painting. "You have a remarkable ability to make the fantastical seem almost tangible. Remember to continue honing your skills and exploring these otherworldly realms."

"Of course, Professor," I said, grateful for his guidance and encouragement.

Over time, my days became a blur of classes, hours spent in the studio refining my skills, and countless sleepless nights as I wrestled with new ideas. My love for Surrealism only grew stronger, fueling my determination to leave an indelible mark on the art world.

"Your dedication is truly impressive, Antonia," remarked Professor Sartori one evening, as he observed me working late in the studio. "But don't forget to balance your drive with moments of rest. Even the greatest artists need time to recharge."

"Thank you for your concern, Professor," I replied, taking a moment to step back from the canvas and analyze my progress. "But I can't help it – there's just so much I want to learn and create."

"Your enthusiasm is commendable," he said with a knowing smile. "Just remember that art is a marathon, not a sprint. Pace yourself, and your talent will undoubtedly flourish."

As I continued my journey through the prestigious halls of the art school, I remained steadfast in my commitment to my craft and the exploration of Surrealism. With each brushstroke, I honed my skills and drew closer to achieving my dreams, driven by my unwavering passion and the guidance of my esteemed professors.

Despite the support and encouragement I received from my professors, I couldn't help but notice the subtle ways in which I was treated differently from my male peers. As one of the few women at the art school, I often found myself on the receiving end of condescending remarks and dismissive attitudes.

"Ah, Antonia," a fellow student, Paulo, once said to me while we were preparing our canvases for a new assignment. "It's good to see you here. It's a shame there aren't more women pursuing their passions, even if they don't have the same natural talent as men."

"Perhaps it's because we face different challenges," I replied with a hint of steel in my voice. "But rest assured, my passion is just as strong, and my talent will prove itself. Now, if you'll excuse me, I have a painting to create."

I clenched my jaw and forced a tight-lipped smile, unwilling to give him the satisfaction of seeing my frustration. Instead, I let my anger fuel my determination, channeling it into my brushstrokes as I threw myself into my work.

I soon discovered that the most effective way to silence my doubters was through the sheer force of my talent. I spent countless hours perfecting my technique and exploring the depths of my creativity, refusing to be deterred by the skepticism of those who believed a woman had no place in the world of art.

As my skills and confidence grew, so too did my reputation within the school. My male peers began to grudgingly respect my abilities, and my professors continued to provide valuable guidance and support.

"Antonia, your latest piece is truly extraordinary," Professor Sartori remarked during a critique session, his eyes shining with admiration. "You've taken the essence of Surrealism and given it a unique, captivating twist. You should be proud of your progress."

"Thank you, Professor," I said, a swell of pride filling my chest. "I couldn't have done it without your guidance and support."

"Your talent and determination are yours alone," he replied with a smile. "It's been an honor to watch you grow as an artist."

In the face of adversity, I refused to let the doubts of others deter me from pursuing my passion. Instead, I harnessed my frustration and channeled it into my work, using it as a catalyst for growth and self-improvement. Through hard work and sheer determination, I overcame the challenges that threatened to hold me back, proving to myself and to the world that I was every bit as deserving of my place in the art world as any man.

As I continued to develop my skills and create exceptional works of art, I became increasingly focused on achieving my ultimate goal: to make a name for myself in the male-dominated art world and demonstrate that a woman's talent and vision could be just as powerful and captivating as any man's. And with each new success, I felt myself drawing closer to that dream – one brushstroke at a time.

The rich scent of oil paint filled my nostrils as I stood before the large canvas, palette in hand. The blank space seemed to beckon me, daring me to bring forth the images that danced in my mind's eye. Surreal art had always been my passion – the way it could challenge and captivate viewers, simultaneously inviting them to question reality and explore the depths of their own subconscious. With a deep breath, I dipped my brush into the vibrant colors on my palette and began to paint.

"Ah, Antonia, there you are," Professor Ricci called out as he entered the studio, his footsteps echoing against the concrete floor. "I've been looking forward to seeing your latest work."

"Hello, Professor," I replied, turning to face him with a smile. "I'm experimenting with some new ideas and techniques. I'm trying to incorporate the essence of Surrealism into my own unique style."

"Excellent!" he exclaimed, his eyes sparkling with genuine enthusiasm. "Surrealism is such a powerful and evocative movement. It's no surprise that it resonates with you."

As the conversation flowed, my brush continued to dance across the canvas, bringing my vision to life with each stroke. My heart pounded with excitement as I merged the fantastical elements of Surrealism with the raw emotion and beauty of my own experiences. Strange landscapes filled with mysterious figures took shape, their distorted forms blending seamlessly with the natural world.

"Look at this," I said, gesturing toward a section of the painting where the roots of a tree morphed into delicate hands reaching for the sky. "I wanted to capture the idea of growth and transformation, but with an otherworldly twist."

"Very intriguing," Professor Ricci mused, studying the piece closely. "You've taken the core principles of Surrealism and infused them with your own personal touch. It's both thought-provoking and visually stunning."

"Thank you," I replied, feeling a blush creep up my cheeks. "Your guidance has been invaluable in helping me to refine my skills and push the boundaries of my creativity."

"Your talent is undeniable, Antonia," he said kindly, placing a hand on my shoulder. "But it's your passion for Surreal art and your determination to make it your own that truly sets you apart."

With renewed vigor, I continued to work on my painting, allowing the essence of Surrealism to guide my brush. The dreamlike images flowed from my mind onto the canvas like a river, each one bearing the distinct mark of my personal style and vision.

As I stood back to admire my creation, I couldn't help but feel a sense of pride and accomplishment. In the face of adversity, I had found solace and inspiration in the world of Surreal art – and in doing so, I had discovered my own unique voice as an artist. With each new piece, I was determined to push the boundaries of what was possible, proving to myself and to the world that a woman's imagination could be just as powerful and enchanting as any man's.

As I entered the grand exhibition hall, a wave of clamoring voices and the scent of fresh oil paint washed over me. The walls were adorned with an array of masterpieces created by my fellow students, their colors vibrant and alive in the dimly lit space. I could feel the weight of expectation bearing down on me as I navigated the room, searching for the perfect spot to display my own creation.

"Ah, Antonia," Professor Deluca greeted me with a knowing smile. "I see you've brought something truly special for this evening's exhibit."

"Thank you, Professor," I replied, clutching my canvas tighter to my chest. "I've poured my heart and soul into this piece, and I hope it will resonate with those who see it."

"Indeed, it is quite the unique vision." He gestured toward an empty easel near the center of the room. "Why don't you set up here? It'll be hard to miss."

With a nod of gratitude, I carefully placed my painting upon the easel, taking a step back to ensure it was level. As I did so, I couldn't help but overhear a group of male students snickering nearby.

"Look at that," one of them sneered, pointing at my work. "A woman trying to make her mark in Surrealism? What's next? A female Cubist?"

"Or a lady Futurist, perhaps?" another chimed in, their laughter growing louder.

"Enough!" I snapped, spinning around to face them. "My gender has no bearing on my talent or creativity. And if you can't appreciate the art for what it is, then perhaps you should take your narrow-minded opinions elsewhere."

The group fell silent, staring at me with wide eyes before they slunk away, leaving me to seethe in indignation. I took several deep breaths, willing my anger to subside, before turning my attention back to the task at hand. This was my moment – my chance to show the world what I was capable of.

As the evening wore on, a steady stream of visitors admired my painting, their expressions shifting from curiosity to awe as they took in the surreal landscape I had crafted. Some even dared to approach me, eager to discuss the symbolism and technique behind my work.

"Your use of color and form is truly remarkable," one woman whispered, her eyes shining with admiration. "You've captured the essence of the subconscious mind in a way I've never seen before."

"Thank you," I murmured, feeling a swell of pride in my chest. "It's been a labor of love, and I hope it will inspire others to explore the boundless possibilities of Surrealist art."

"Of that, I have no doubt," she replied, offering a warm smile before moving on to the next exhibit.

As the night drew to a close, I found myself standing alone beside my piece, lost in thought. The faces of those who had admired my work throughout the evening seemed to blur together, each one representing a small victory against the stifling constraints of societal expectation.

Tonight, I had proven that my talent could shine through, even in the face of adversity. But I knew there was still much work to be done.

One day, I vowed to myself, I would make a name for Antonia Pageta not just as a female Surrealist artist, but as a visionary who pushed the boundaries of perception and reality. And when that day came, the world would remember me not for my gender, but for the power and beauty of my creations.

The following morning, I entered the grand halls of the prestigious art school with renewed determination. Sunlight filtered through the ornate windows, casting intricate patterns on the marble floors and illuminating the works of art that adorned the walls. It was here, amidst the echoes of greatness, where I would forge my path.

"Ah, Antonia," Professor Marino greeted me as I arrived at his studio for our scheduled critique. He was a stern, silver-haired man with an eye for detail and a reputation for pushing his students to their limits. "Let's see what progress you've made."

I carefully unrolled my latest creation, a large canvas covered in a swirl of colors and shapes that seemed to dance before the eyes. Professor Marino studied it intently, his brow furrowed in concentration.

"Your use of color is striking, your technique shows promise," he finally said, locking eyes with me. "But remember, Antonia, Surrealism is not just about the visual impact. It's about exploring the depths of the subconscious mind and creating a connection between dreams and reality."

"I understand, Professor," I replied, nodding vigorously. "I'll work on incorporating more symbolism into my pieces, delving deeper into the world of dreams."

"Good. Don't be afraid to take risks," he encouraged me, softening slightly. "You have a unique perspective, and if you can harness it, you'll achieve great things."

As the weeks went by, I threw myself into my studies with unyielding passion. I attended lectures on the history of art, honing my understanding of the movements that had come before me. In the library, I pored over books detailing the techniques of the masters, absorbing every word like a sponge.

In the evenings, I retreated to my small studio, surrounded by the scent of oil paint and turpentine. There, I pushed the boundaries of my imagination, experimenting with new ideas and challenging myself to go beyond the confines of what I thought was possible.

"Antonia, this piece is truly remarkable," Professor Benci, a renowned art historian, said one day as he examined my latest work. "You've captured the essence of the Surrealist movement while adding your own unique touch."

"Thank you, Professor," I responded, my heart swelling with pride. "I've been working hard to find my voice within the movement."

"Keep going, Antonia. Your dedication and talent will take you far," he encouraged me, his eyes twinkling with excitement. "And when the time comes, don't be afraid to make your mark on the world."

As the semesters passed, I continued to grow as an artist, refining my skills and expanding my knowledge under the watchful eyes of my professors. With each critique, each word of encouragement, I felt myself inching closer to achieving my goals—to making a name for Antonia Pageta in the art world, and leaving an indelible mark on the history of Surrealism.

With graduation on the horizon, I knew that the next chapter of my life was about to begin. And as I stood at the threshold of greatness, I couldn't help but feel a surge of anticipation for what the future held.

"Remember, Antonia," Professor Marino's words echoed in my mind as I packed away my brushes and paints, preparing to leave the hallowed halls of the prestigious art school behind. "The world awaits your vision. Now, go forth and show them what you're capable of."

With determination burning in my soul, I stepped out into the sunlight, ready to face the challenges ahead and carve my name into the annals of art history. The world would soon know the name Antonia Pageta—and they would never forget it.

CHAPTER 4

The scent of oil paint and turpentine filled the air as I dipped my brush into a swirl of colors on my palette. My eyes wandered over the canvas, searching for the perfect spot to place the next stroke. Surrealism was my way of revealing the hidden truths of life, and each painting was a piece of my soul exposed to the world. My name is Antonia Pageta, and I am an artist.

"Antonia!" called my mother, Silvia, from downstairs. "Your father will be home soon, and you know how he feels about your art."

I sighed and put down my brush, knowing she was right. Father had never understood my passion for art. He was a traditional man, believing in hard work and providing for one's family. To him, my paintings were nothing more than a frivolous hobby. But to me, they were my lifeline.

"Coming, Mama," I replied. I took one last look at my canvas before reluctantly leaving my sanctuary.

My mother met me at the bottom of the stairs with a warm embrace. "Your talent is a gift, Antonia, but sometimes it makes life difficult," she said softly.

"I know, Mama. But I can't stop painting. It's who I am."

"Of course not, my love. Just be patient with your father. He only wants what's best for you."

As if on cue, my father, Maurizio, walked through the door, his heavy boots thudding against the floor. His eyes immediately locked onto mine. "Antonia, we need to talk," he said firmly.

"Can it wait, Papa? I'm working on something important."

"Your future is more important," he replied, leading me to the kitchen table. "Antonia, I've arranged for you to work at your Uncle's bakery. It's time you start thinking about a real career."

"Father, I already have a real career. I am an artist!"

"Art doesn't pay the bills, Antonia," he said, his voice raising. "You need to be practical and start thinking about your future."

"Art is my future, Papa! You know how much it means to me," I pleaded.

"Enough!" he bellowed, slamming his fist on the table. "You will work at the bakery, and that's final!"

As tears filled my eyes, I knew this was just one of the many challenges I would face in my pursuit of a life dedicated to art. My father may never understand my passion, but I couldn't let him dictate my life. My journey as a surrealist artist was only just beginning, and I had yet to face the obstacles of the art world itself. But through it all, I would remain fiercely independent and true to my creative vision, no matter the cost.

Months had passed since that fateful day with my father, and my life had taken an unexpected turn. I found myself working at the bakery, kneading dough instead of painting on canvas. The scent of freshly baked bread hovered in the air as I toiled away, each loaf a bitter reminder of my dreams being stifled.

"Antonia, make sure these loaves are shaped perfectly!" Uncle Marco barked from across the kitchen. "We've got customers waiting!"

"Of course, Uncle," I replied through gritted teeth, forcing a smile as I continued to form the dough into perfect circles.

As the weeks went by, I couldn't shake the feeling that I was wasting away, my creative spirit starving for nourishment. Late at night, after the bakery closed, I would sneak into my makeshift studio - a corner of my tiny bedroom - and lose myself in my paintings. With every stroke of my brush, I felt alive again, my soul soaring as I created worlds only I could see.

"Antonia, you look exhausted," my friend Giovanni said one evening as we sat at a small cafe downtown. "Are you still painting late into the night?"

I hesitated before answering, fearful of judgment. "Yes," I admitted, staring down at my coffee. "Art is the only thing that makes me feel truly alive, Giovanni. How can I give that up?"

He reached out, placing his hand on mine, his eyes warm and understanding. "You shouldn't have to, Antonia. You're talented, and your passion for your art is inspiring. Don't let anyone take that away from you."

His words struck a chord deep within me, igniting a fire in my heart. In that moment, I knew I couldn't let my love for art be smothered by others' expectations. My journey wouldn't be easy, but I needed to stand up for myself and my vision.

"Thank you," I said, my voice steady with newfound determination. "I promise you, I won't let anyone hold me back."

The very next day, I stood before my father and Uncle Marco, my heart pounding in my chest as I mustered up every ounce of courage I possessed.

"Father, Uncle, I cannot continue working at the bakery," I declared, my voice unwavering. "I appreciate the opportunity, but my heart belongs to my art. I must pursue my dreams, even if it means defying your wishes."

Their faces betrayed a mix of shock and disappointment, but I held my ground. I knew this was the first step toward reclaiming my destiny, toward becoming the artist I was always meant to be. And from that moment on, I vowed never to compromise my creative vision or let fear dictate the course of my life.

-

The morning sun illuminated the cobblestone streets of Milan as I walked towards my first job as a fashion model. It was an opportunity that fell into my lap, completely unexpected, but one I couldn't ignore. Taking a deep breath, I pushed open the heavy glass doors to the luxurious studio and stepped inside.

"Ah, Antonia! You're finally here!" A woman in a crisp white blouse and black pencil skirt greeted me, her eyes scanning my face with an intensity that made me feel both flattered and exposed. "Have a seat over there, and we'll get started right away."

"Thank you," I replied softly, trying to hide my nerves as I took in my surroundings. The studio was filled with bright lights and cameras, makeup artists, hair stylists, and wardrobe assistants bustling around, focused on their tasks.

"Antonia, right?" A makeup artist named Francesca approached me, holding a brush in one hand and a palette of colors in the other. "I've heard great things about you. Excited for your first shoot?"

"Excited and nervous," I admitted, watching as she skillfully applied foundation to my face. I had always been drawn to art, particularly surrealism, and I wondered if I could bring some of that creativity to this new venture of mine.

"Trust me, you'll do amazing. You have such a unique look." She smiled reassuringly before moving on to my eye makeup.

As I sat in the chair, looking at my reflection in the mirror, I felt a rush of uncertainty. Was this really where I wanted to be? But then, I remembered the village I came from, and how fiercely determined I was to create a life for myself beyond its borders.

"Alright, Antonia, we're ready for you on set!" The photographer called out.

"Good luck," Francesca whispered as she put the finishing touches on my hair.

"Thank you," I replied, my heart racing as I stood up and made my way to the center of the studio. The bright lights were blinding, but I forced myself to focus and strike a pose.

"Beautiful! Just like that!" The photographer encouraged me as he snapped photo after photo. I could feel their eyes on me, analyzing every move I made, every angle of my face and body.

"Antonia, try looking off to the side, as if you're lost in thought." The photographer directed me, and I complied, trying to channel my love for surrealism and the endless possibilities it represented.

"Perfect!" He exclaimed, capturing the moment with his camera. "You truly are a natural."

As I continued to pose, dressed in exquisite garments I had only ever dreamed of wearing, I couldn't shake the feeling that something was missing. Was this glamorous world of fashion truly where I belonged? Or was there something more meaningful waiting for me, just beyond my reach?

Only time would tell.

The camera flashed once more before the photographer lowered it, a satisfied smile playing on his lips. "Magnifico," he declared, stepping out from behind the lens to reveal his handsome features and stylishly tousled brown hair. "I am Enzo Romano," he introduced himself, extending a hand for me to shake.

"Antonia Pageta," I replied, my voice steady despite the sudden thudding in my chest. Enzo's reputation preceded him. His captivating fashion photography graced the pages of the most prestigious magazines, and I knew that working with him could open doors for me in the industry.

"Your beauty is truly extraordinary, Antonia," Enzo said, his dark eyes appraising me as if I were one of his subjects. "You have a unique presence in front of the camera. The potential to make a real impact in the world of fashion."

"Thank you," I murmured, his compliments stirring a mixture of flattery and unease within me. I was a surrealist artist at heart, and while I appreciated the artistry of fashion, I couldn't help but wonder if it aligned with my true passions and beliefs.

"Come, let me show you something," Enzo beckoned, leading me to a table covered with large prints of his work. As I examined the stunning images before me, I marveled at the way he captured the essence of each model, transforming them into ethereal creatures that seemed to exist in a realm beyond our own.

"Your work is incredible," I breathed, unable to tear my eyes away from the photos. Enzo's talent was undeniable, and part of me longed to be immortalized through his lens.

"Imagine yourself here, Antonia," Enzo said softly, tracing a finger along the edge of a particularly striking image. "With your unique beauty and presence, we could create something truly unforgettable."

His words sent a shiver down my spine, the temptation to embrace this glamorous world growing stronger. Yet, as I glanced back at the bustling studio, I couldn't shake the nagging feeling that something vital was missing — a sense of purpose, perhaps.

"Think about it, Antonia," Enzo murmured, his gaze locked on mine. "Together, we could create magic."

I hesitated, my mind racing with conflicting emotions. The opportunity to work with someone as talented as Enzo was not one to be taken lightly, but did it align with my true desires? Would I find fulfillment in this world, or would I always be searching for something more?

"Thank you, Enzo," I replied finally, forcing a smile. "Your words mean a lot to me. I'll definitely consider it."

"Good," he said, nodding approvingly. "I have a feeling you're destined for great things, Antonia."

As we returned to the set, I couldn't help but wonder if those great things lay within the dazzling world of fashion or beyond its glittering facade. The answer remained elusive, but one thing was certain: I wouldn't stop until I found it.

The glare of the studio lights seemed almost blinding as I hesitated at the edge of the set. The air was thick with the scent of hairspray and the sound of hurried footsteps echoed through the room. I stole a glance at Enzo, who stood poised by his camera, waiting for me to make a decision.

"Antonia," he said softly, sensing my apprehension. "Trust me. You have an incredible gift, one that should be shared with the world."

I bit my lip, torn between the allure of this glamorous life and the uncertainty that weighed heavily on my heart. "Enzo, it's not that I don't appreciate the opportunity, but... I just don't know if this is the right path for me. Modeling feels so superficial. It doesn't seem to hold any real meaning."

Enzo leaned against the camera, his eyes never leaving mine. "Antonia, the modeling industry may have its flaws, but it can also be a powerful platform for change. Just imagine the impact you could have – the people you could inspire."

A flicker of excitement ignited within me at the thought, but it was quickly extinguished by doubt. "But what about the pressure to maintain a certain image? To constantly strive for an unattainable perfection?"

"Perfection is overrated," Enzo replied with a dismissive wave of his hand. "What truly matters is authenticity. And believe me, you possess that in spades."

I sighed, running my fingers through my hair as I considered his words. He had a point – perhaps there was more to this industry than met the eye. And working with someone as talented as Enzo would undoubtedly be a once-in-a-lifetime experience.

"Alright, Enzo," I agreed, swallowing my lingering reservations. "Let's give this a shot."

A triumphant smile spread across his face as he clapped his hands together. "Excellent! Trust me, Antonia, you won't regret this."

As I stepped onto the set, my heart hammered in my chest, both from nerves and a flicker of excitement at the prospect of what lay ahead. And though uncertainty still lingered in the back of my mind, I couldn't help but feel a thrill at the idea of exploring this new world and discovering where it might lead.

"Ah, Antonia! You're a natural!" Enzo exclaimed as he expertly snapped photographs of me from various angles. The lights surrounding the set were harsh and bright, but I found that my initial hesitation was slowly melting away under Enzo's enthusiastic guidance.

"Turn slightly to your left," he instructed, his eyes never leaving the camera lens. "Yes, just like that. Perfect."

I shifted my weight onto my other foot and tilted my head, following his direction. The fabric of the elegant gown I wore swished around my legs, making me feel like a princess in some far-off fairytale.

"Remember to breathe," Enzo reminded me with a gentle smile. "You're doing wonderfully."

Inhaling deeply, I allowed myself to truly focus on the moment. The camera shutter clicked rapidly, capturing each subtle movement I made. As the shoot progressed, I began to feel more and more at ease, settling into a rhythm of posing and expressing myself through my body.

"Let's try a new outfit!" Enzo suggested after a while, his excitement contagious. I retreated to the changing area, where a team of assistants eagerly helped me slip into one breathtaking ensemble after another. From flowing gowns to structured suits, each outfit seemed to accentuate my beauty and grace in a different way.

"Alright, this time, I want you to channel your inner strength," Enzo called out as I emerged in a bold red dress, my confidence growing with each passing moment.

I took a deep breath, drawing upon the same resilience and determination that had carried me through my artistic journey thus far. As I struck a power pose, my fingers clenching the fabric of my dress, I could see Enzo's eyes widen in admiration.

"Brilliant, Antonia! Absolutely brilliant!" he praised, snapping photo after photo as my inner fire burned brighter. "You've got something truly special, you know."

His words sent a warmth through my chest that I hadn't felt in a long time – the thrill of being seen and appreciated for who I truly was. And though I still harbored doubts about the world of fashion modeling, I couldn't deny that working with Enzo had opened my eyes to possibilities I'd never considered before.

"Last outfit," Enzo announced after some more shots, his voice tinged with a hint of sadness. "But don't worry, Antonia. This is just the beginning. You're going to do incredible things."

As I posed in the final ensemble, a chic black pantsuit that made me feel both powerful and elegant, I couldn't help but wonder if he was right. Could there be a place for me in this world, where authenticity and self-expression were valued above all else? Or was I simply getting swept away by the glamour and allure of it all?

"Thank you, Enzo," I murmured as the shoot drew to a close, my heart heavy with conflicting emotions. "For everything."

"Of course, my dear," he replied, flashing me one last dazzling smile. "Now go out there and show the world what you're made of."

Upon leaving the studio, I felt the weight of my surroundings – the blinding lights, the cameras, and the ever-watchful eyes of the fashion industry that seemed to scrutinize every inch of me. The air outside was crisp and cool, a sharp contrast to the stifling atmosphere within. As I walked aimlessly through the bustling streets of Milan, I couldn't shake an unsettling feeling in the pit of my stomach.

"Antonia," a voice called out, breaking my train of thought. It was Francesca, the makeup artist from the shoot. "You did amazing today! You're a natural."

"Thank you," I replied, forcing a smile. But her words only deepened my discomfort as I began to question the meaning behind all the praise and admiration. Was it truly for me, Antonia, the person who had grown up in a small village with dreams of becoming an artist? Or was it for the image I now portrayed – the beautiful, graceful model who existed only within the confines of a magazine page?

"Are you alright?" Francesca asked, a note of concern in her voice. "You seem...distracted."

"I'm just thinking about some things," I admitted, hesitant to reveal my growing unease about the modeling world. I glanced at the lively city around us, watching people hurry past without a second glance, their lives driven by ambition and desire. And suddenly, I found myself longing for something more – something deeper and more meaningful than the superficiality that seemed to pervade this world I'd stumbled into.

"Francesca," I said softly, "do you think there's more to life than just being beautiful?"

"Of course," she responded, furrowing her brow in confusion. "Beauty is just one aspect of life. There's so much more to explore and experience."

Her words resonated with me, stirring a dormant passion within my soul. I thought back to my love for painting, the way my art could transport me to other worlds and allow me to connect with others on a deeper level. And then there were my passions for social justice and making a difference in the world – ideals that seemed so far removed from the vanity and self-indulgence of the fashion industry.

"Francesca," I whispered, my voice trembling with newfound determination, "I think I need to find a different path. One that aligns with who I truly am and what I believe in."

She looked at me for a moment, her eyes searching mine before finally nodding in understanding. "You have to follow your heart, Antonia. That's the only way to find true happiness."

With her encouragement, I felt a sense of clarity wash over me as I resolved to forge my own path in life, one filled with purpose and meaning. The glamour and allure of the modeling world may have been tempting, but it was time for me to embrace my true passions and pursue a life that reflected my values and interests. And as I walked away from the glittering lights of Milan, I knew that despite the uncertainty that lay ahead, I was finally headed in the right direction.

As I stood in the dimly lit hallway outside the studio, my heart heavy with the weight of my decision, Enzo appeared from around the corner. His eyes sparkled like polished onyx as he flashed me a warm smile.

"Antonia, I've been looking for you," he said, his voice smooth as silk. "I wanted to talk to you about something important."

"Sure, Enzo," I replied, my voice wavering ever so slightly, betraying the unease that gnawed at my insides.

"Listen, cara," he began, leaning against the wall with a casual grace that seemed effortlessly cool. "I know you have your doubts about this industry, but I think you have a real future here. You're talented and beautiful, and there's no telling how far you could go."

His words washed over me like an ocean wave, and I could sense the genuine admiration behind them. But deep down, I knew that I couldn't stay in this world any longer – not when my heart yearned for something more meaningful.

"Enzo, I appreciate your kind words, but I've realized that this just isn't the right path for me."

He looked at me incredulously, as if I had just told him the sky was green. "Antonia, don't be hasty. I can introduce you to some of the biggest names in fashion. There are countless opportunities waiting for you if you stick with it."

I sighed, feeling the pull of temptation threatening to sway me from my resolve. "It's not about the connections or the opportunities, Enzo. This world doesn't align with what truly matters to me."

"Then what does?" he pressed, his dark eyes probing mine for answers.

"I want to make a difference in the world through painting and advocating for social justice," I confessed, my chest swelling with the passion that fueled my desire for change. "I can't do that while posing in front of a camera."

For a moment, Enzo seemed to consider my words before nodding slowly. "I understand," he admitted reluctantly, his voice tinged with disappointment. "But just remember, Antonia – the door is always open if you change your mind."

"Thank you, Enzo," I whispered, feeling a bittersweet mix of gratitude and sadness as I hugged him goodbye. As I walked away from the glamorous world that had seduced me, I knew that this was the beginning of a new chapter in my life – one where I could finally pursue my dreams with authenticity and conviction.

CHAPTER 5

The cold, gray streets of Paris seemed to shiver as I walked in the rain, clutching my portfolio tightly against my chest. My name is Antonia Pageta, and I am a surrealist artist in the 1940s, fighting to make a name for myself in a world that seems determined to ignore me. I have always been driven by an unyielding desire to prove myself, to show the world that my art is worth their attention - that I am worth their attention. But it is not easy being a woman in this male-dominated field, especially one who has been cursed with beauty.

"Mademoiselle, your paintings are... interesting," said the gallery owner as he glanced distractedly at my works, his eyes flickering between my face and the canvases I had poured my soul into. "But perhaps they would be better suited for a different venue."

"Is it because they are too avant-garde for your taste?" I asked, trying to keep the bitterness from seeping into my voice. He shook his head, a hint of condescension creeping into his smile.

"Non, non, it is simply that I believe our clientele is more accustomed to traditional styles, and while your art is undoubtedly unique, I fear it would not sell well here." I could see the unspoken words lingering in the air between us: it was not just my art that was undesirable, but me, a woman whose beauty seemed to be both a blessing and a curse in equal measure.

I fought back the sting of tears as I left the gallery, feeling the weight of discrimination pressing down on me like a heavy cloud. It was a constant battle to try and make people see past my appearance, to recognize the talent and passion that burned within me. I knew that some of the men who dismissed my work so casually would likely be enchanted by my looks if we were to meet outside the confines of the art world, but it was a hollow comfort.

"Antonia!" called a familiar voice as I trudged through the rain, and I looked up to see my mother, Silvia, standing in the doorway of our small Parisian apartment. She held her arms open wide, ready to embrace me and offer solace. "Come inside, carissima," she urged, and I gratefully accepted her warmth, longing for the comfort that only a mother's love could provide.

"Another rejection?" asked my father, Maurizio, as he peered at me from behind his newspaper, his gruff exterior hiding a tenderness that he seldom allowed to show. I nodded silently, my heart heavy with disappointment.

"Never mind them, Antonia," said my mother, her voice soft and soothing. "You are a brilliant artist, and one day they will all see what we have always known."

I smiled weakly, knowing that she believed her words with every fiber of her being. But as I sat down to dinner with my loving family, I couldn't help but wonder: would the world ever truly appreciate my art? Or would I forever be judged not on the merit of my work, but on the whims and prejudices of those who refused to look past my appearance?

As I stared down at my plate, lost in my thoughts, I vowed that no matter how many times they tried to tear me down, I would continue to fight, to push forward, and to create. Because I am Antonia Pageta, surrealist artist, and I will not be silenced.

The sun had barely risen, casting a soft golden light through the cracks of my rickety studio window. I could feel its warmth on my face, beckoning me to face the day and lose myself in the world I created with each stroke of my paintbrush. The smell of turpentine and oil paints filled the air as I surveyed my latest piece, a canvas teeming with fluid shapes and a dreamscape that whispered secrets only I could understand.

"Ah, Antonia, still wasting your time with these frivolous paintings?" The voice slithered into my sanctuary like a snake, making me shudder with disgust. I turned to find Helmut Schmidt leaning against the doorframe, his smug smile twisting his features into a cruel mockery of a man who claimed to appreciate art. As one of the most influential critics in the art world, his words held the power to make or break an artist's career.

"Good morning, Mr. Schmidt," I replied coolly, refusing to allow him to diminish my spirits. "I didn't expect to see you here."

"Surprised?" he chuckled darkly. "It is my responsibility to keep an eye on all potential artists, even those who don't quite fit the mold." His gaze lingered upon my body, his intentions clear.

"Your visits are always so enlightening," I retorted, gritting my teeth as I dipped my brush into a vibrant shade of blue. "But if you'll excuse me, I have work to do."

"Very well," he conceded, stepping back but not leaving entirely. "I shall observe from a distance. I wouldn't want to disrupt your precious process."

With a deep breath, I did my best to ignore his presence and focus on the painting before me. My hands danced across the canvas, guided by intuition rather than any predetermined plan. I allowed the colors to speak to me, weaving them together to create a world where my imagination could run free. Surreal figures emerged from the depths of my subconscious, their forms twisting and melding with the landscape as I sought to capture the essence of my dreams.

"Interesting," Helmut muttered, his voice dripping with condescension. "But hardly groundbreaking."

"Art is not about breaking ground, Mr. Schmidt," I responded without looking up from my work. "It's about exploring the depths of our minds and inviting others to do the same."

"Perhaps," he sneered, "but it seems you have much exploring left to do before your work can be taken seriously. You are a woman, after all, and a beautiful one at that. How can you expect anyone to believe there is depth beneath that pretty face?"

His words stung like a slap across my cheek, but I refused to let him see the pain they caused. Instead, I held my head high and continued to paint, allowing the colors to become an extension of my defiance.

"Perhaps it is you who lacks depth, Mr. Schmidt," I said, my voice steady and unwavering. "For if you cannot recognize the beauty in what lies beyond the surface, then you are truly blind."

And with that final stroke, I signed my name to the canvas, sealing my fate as an artist who would never bow to the likes of Helmut Schmidt.

The room hummed with the steady rhythm of my paintbrush as I dabbed the bristles into a palette of bold, unorthodox colors. My heart beat wildly in my chest, pushing me to explore new depths within myself and my art. I felt the urge to experiment, to push the boundaries of traditional artistic norms that the likes of Helmut Schmidt sought to enforce.

"Antonia," my friend Carla called from across the studio, "what are you working on? It's so...different."

"Exactly," I replied, a smile playing on my lips. "I am attempting to create something that defies expectation, something that will make people question what they think they know about art." I paused, studying the canvas before me. "And perhaps it will also challenge their preconceived notions about who can be an artist."

Carla approached the easel, her eyes wide as she took in the chaotic fusion of colors and shapes. She hesitated for a moment before asking, "But will this be enough to gain recognition in a world that seems dead set against you?"

"Recognition isn't everything," I said, though the weight of constant rejection stung like a thousand paper cuts. "What matters most is staying true to my vision and not allowing others' narrow-mindedness to dictate what I create."

"Your determination is admirable, Antonia," Carla said, placing a hand on my shoulder. "I just worry that it may not be enough to overcome the obstacles placed before you."

"Perhaps not," I admitted, my brush pausing mid-stroke, "but I refuse to let fear or discrimination hold me back. No matter how many rejections I face, no matter how many times my work is criticized, I will continue to paint, to grow, and to push the limits of artistic expression."

With renewed vigor, I returned to my canvas, blending my defiance and resilience into each brushstroke. This was my journey, and it was one that I would never abandon, no matter the challenges that lay ahead.

The scent of fresh oil paints and turpentine invaded my senses as I stepped into the dimly lit studio. Canvases lined the walls, their vibrant colors battling the encroaching shadows. My heart raced with anticipation; tonight, I would unveil my latest creation to a small circle of friends and fellow artists. It was an opportunity for them to witness the progress I'd made despite the countless setbacks that sought to break me. The smallest crack in the door could be the beginning of something greater.

"Antonia, this piece is extraordinary!" exclaimed Giovanni, an old friend and fellow artist, who approached the painting with wide eyes.

"Thank you," I replied, my chest swelling with pride. "I wanted to push myself even further, to weave together a dreamscape that challenges the viewer's perception of reality."

"Your determination has paid off," he said, studying the intricate details of the surreal landscape. "This might just be the breakthrough you've been waiting for."

"Perhaps," I said, trying not to get my hopes up too high. "But regardless, I will continue to create and share my art with the world."

"Brava, Antonia," another voice chimed in. It was Rosa, an esteemed art critic known for her unyielding standards. "You've managed to capture the essence of surrealism in a way that is both captivating and thought-provoking."

"Thank you, Rosa," I said, my heart pounding louder with each passing moment. Could this be the turning point I had been longing for?

"Your work deserves more recognition than it receives," she continued, examining the painting closely. "And I intend to make sure it gets it. With your permission, I would like to write a feature on your art for the next issue of 'L'Esprit Artistique.'"

"Of course! I would be honored," I stammered, my mind racing with the thought of my art gracing the pages of such an esteemed publication.

"Then it's settled," Rosa said, offering me a warm smile. "It's time the world became acquainted with the brilliant and groundbreaking work of Antonia Pageta."

As the night wore on, I felt a renewed sense of hope and determination take root within me. The struggle had been long and arduous, but the faint glimmer of recognition now illuminated my path. It was only the beginning - but a promising one, at last.

I stood before the canvas, brush in hand, as a group of eager young art students watched my every stroke. They had come to my studio seeking guidance, and I was more than happy to share my passion with them. My newfound recognition had opened doors for me, and I was now able to inspire others to pursue their own passions.

"Observe how I blend the colors," I instructed, the vibrant hues swirling together like a dream. "Surrealism is about defying conventional norms and embracing your own perspective."

"I've always wanted to try something like this," whispered a young girl named Maria, her eyes wide with admiration. "But I was afraid people might laugh at me."

"Never let fear hold you back," I told her, recalling my own struggles against discrimination. "Your voice is unique and valuable; embrace it with confidence."

As I continued to paint, I shared anecdotes of my past experiences - the countless rejections, the snide remarks made by men who deemed me unworthy because of my gender and beauty. The students listened intently, each absorbing the tale of my perseverance as they began to realize that they, too, could overcome any obstacles in their path.

"Antonia, how did you find the strength to keep going when everything seemed stacked against you?" asked a tall, lanky boy named Pietro.

"By believing in myself and my work," I replied. "And by surrounding myself with those who believed in me, too."

I gestured to the various paintings adorning the walls of my studio, each one a testament to my artistic expression and an act of defiance against those who sought to suppress it. The students gazed upon them in awe, taking in the surreal landscapes and ethereal figures that danced across the canvas.

"Your art truly speaks for itself," said Maria, her voice filled with wonder. "Thank you for showing us what's possible when we stay true to our vision."

"Your art will speak for you, too," I assured her. "You must simply have the courage to share it with the world."

As the students departed, I felt a warm sense of pride and satisfaction. My journey had been fraught with challenges and setbacks, but by persevering and staying true to my artistic expression, I had not only gained recognition for my work but also become a symbol of hope and perseverance for others.

"Antonia Pageta!" called out Helmut Schmidt, entering my studio unannounced. "Seems like your newfound fame has inspired a whole new generation of artists."

"Indeed, Helmut," I replied, my tone resolute. "And I will continue to inspire and empower those who dare to dream, no matter what barriers they face."

"Bravo!" he said sarcastically. "But remember, Antonia, there's always someone waiting to take your place."

"Perhaps," I conceded. "But let them come. My art has given me the strength to overcome far greater obstacles than mere competition."

The sun dipped low in the sky, casting its golden light across the city as I walked through the bustling streets. The scent of freshly baked bread and brewing coffee filled my nostrils as I passed by cafes and bakeries, while laughter and the chatter of conversation rose like a symphony all around me.

"Signora Pageta," a young artist named Pietro called out to me, catching up with a sketchbook in hand. "Your latest exhibition has inspired me to experiment with new mediums and styles. May I show you?"

"Of course," I replied, my heart swelling with pride. As I perused his pages, I marveled at the vibrancy and freedom of his lines, the boldness of his colors. It was evident that he had been emboldened by my work, and it filled me with joy.

"Keep pushing those boundaries, Pietro," I encouraged him, patting him on the back before we parted ways.

I entered my studio, feeling the cool air wash over me as I shut the door and left the clamor of the outside world behind. My sanctuary awaited me, a space where I could pour my very soul onto canvas. Paintbrushes stood like soldiers in their jars, and half-finished canvases leered from the walls, hungry for completion.

As I began to mix my paints, my mind wandered to the discrimination that still plagued my journey. How many times had Helmut Schmidt and his ilk scoffed at my work? Dismissed me because of my gender or beauty? But it was that adversity that fueled my determination to prove my worth as an artist – and as a woman.

"Let them underestimate me," I whispered to myself, beginning to paint with fervent strokes. "They cannot break me."

My fingers danced across the canvas, my paintbrush a conductor's baton orchestrating a symphony of color and form. I wove together dreamscapes and memories, creating a world where the fantastical and the mundane were intertwined.

"Antonia," I thought to myself, "you have come so far, and there is still so much more to do."

I stepped back from my latest creation, the colors still wet and gleaming on the canvas. A smile spread across my face as I imagined the possibilities that lay ahead. No matter what challenges awaited me, I would continue to forge my own path in the art world, inspiring others along the way.

"Helmut Schmidt may try to tear me down," I said softly, looking at my reflection in a nearby mirror. "But I will not falter. My art will speak for itself, and my voice will be heard."

The sun dipped below the horizon, casting my studio in a warm, golden glow. As darkness began to fall outside, I knew that no shadow could extinguish the light within me. With determination in my heart and paintbrush in hand, I was ready to face whatever the world had in store.

CHAPTER 6

I found myself walking down a cobblestone alleyway, the sun casting its warm golden light on the ancient stonework. It was on this path that I often met with my two closest friends - Enzo Romano and Giovanni Bellini. One was my lover, the other my confidante. Together, we formed an odd triangle.

Enzo's strides were long and confident as he approached me, his hands tucked into his tailored pants pockets. As always, he exuded charm, with his wavy dark hair effortlessly styled and his deep green eyes sparkling with mischief. "Antonia, bella" he greeted me, pressing a soft kiss onto my cheek. His lips lingered for a moment longer than necessary, and I felt a flush creep up my neck. "I have some exciting news about a new photo project. You'll be perfect for it."

"Buongiorno, Enzo," I replied, trying to keep my voice steady. "Tell me more about this project of yours."

As Enzo launched into a detailed explanation of the project, I couldn't help but notice Giovanni lingering in the background. Unlike Enzo, Giovanni was a quiet, steadfast presence in my life. He wore paint-splattered clothes, evidence of his dedication to his craft, and his brown eyes were filled with warmth and understanding. We had grown up together, sharing our dreams of becoming renowned artists. Our friendship was a safety net, a comfort in times of turmoil.

"Antonia, are you listening?" Enzo asked, pulling me out of my thoughts.

"Of course, Enzo," I said, forcing a smile. He went on to explain that a prestigious fashion magazine was looking for a surrealistic cover image, and he was sure that my paintings would make the perfect backdrop for his photography. It sounded like a great opportunity, but something about the way he described the project made me uneasy. I couldn't shake the feeling that he was more focused on promoting his own career than helping mine.

"Enzo, I'm flattered, but are you sure they're interested in my work? It sounds like this is more about your photography." I hesitated, watching Enzo's face for any signs of disappointment or frustration.

"Antonia," Enzo said, placing a hand on my shoulder. "Trust me, this will be great for both of us. Your art will be seen by millions, and we'll both become famous."

As much as I wanted to believe him, I couldn't help but remember the times Enzo had steered me towards projects that seemed to benefit him more than me. There was the time he insisted on photographing me for an exhibition, only to have the photos overshadow my paintings. And then there was the gallery owner who Enzo had introduced me to, promising that she would be smitten with my work. Instead, she'd spent the entire evening fawning over Enzo and discussing potential collaborations with him.

"Let me think about it, Enzo," I finally said, trying to keep my voice steady.

"Of course, Antonia," he replied, his eyes softening. "Take all the time you need. I'm sure you'll make the right decision." The smile he gave me seemed sincere, but I knew it masked a manipulative streak that lurked beneath the surface.

As Enzo walked away, Giovanni approached, his concern evident in his furrowed brow. He didn't need to say anything; our shared history spoke volumes. We stood together in the fading light, the sun casting its final golden rays on the cobblestones, as I pondered the choices before me.

"Enzo is so charming, isn't he?" I mused aloud, watching him as he chatted with a group of admirers near the entrance to the gallery. The man had an undeniable magnetism that drew people towards him, like moths to a flame.

"Indeed," Giovanni agreed, his tone cautious. "But charm can be dangerous, Antonia. Remember, it's not always what it seems."

I sighed and glanced at my friend, who was wearing a look of concern that I'd come to know all too well. "You worry too much, Giovanni. Enzo has been nothing but supportive of my art. He believes in me."

"Does he, though?" Giovanni asked gently, taking my hand in his. "Or does he just see your talent as something he can use for his own gain?"

My heart clenched at the suggestion, but I couldn't deny the truth in Giovanni's words. Enzo's ambitious streak could sometimes make me question his motives. Yet, I found myself drawn to him in spite of this - or perhaps because of it. His confidence and drive were intoxicating, and when he looked at me with those smoldering eyes, it was hard to remember any doubts I had about him.

"Even if that's true, I can handle Enzo," I insisted, pulling my hand away from Giovanni's gentle grasp. "Besides, he's helped me get my work out there. Without him, I wouldn't have gotten half the recognition I have now."

"Recognition isn't everything, my friend," Giovanni replied, his voice soft and steady. "It's your passion and dedication to your craft that truly matter. Don't lose sight of that in pursuit of fame."

"Look, I appreciate your concern," I said, trying to keep frustration from creeping into my voice. "But Enzo and I are a team. We're good for each other. I just need to trust him."

Giovanni studied me for a moment, his warm brown eyes filled with empathy. "Alright, Antonia," he said finally. "Just know that I'm here for you, no matter what. If you ever need someone to talk to or a shoulder to lean on, you can always count on me."

"Thank you, Giovanni," I replied, touched by his unwavering loyalty. "I promise, if anything ever goes wrong, you'll be the first person I turn to."

"Good," he said, nodding and offering me a small smile. "Now, let's enjoy this gallery opening of yours, shall we? You've worked so hard for this moment, and you deserve to bask in its glory."

Giovanni's support meant the world to me, and as we wandered through the gallery together, admiring the surreal landscapes and dreamlike figures that adorned the walls, I couldn't help but feel grateful for our friendship. As much as Enzo brought excitement and opportunity into my life, it was Giovanni's steadfast love and understanding that truly kept me grounded.

As the months rolled on, the excitement and opportunity that Enzo brought into my life began to wane. His charm and charisma were shadowed by his manipulative tendencies, making our relationship tumultuous. In the midst of this turmoil, I found solace in my conversations with Giovanni.

One evening, after yet another disagreement with Enzo about which magazine would be best for showcasing my artwork, I called Giovanni, tears streaming down my face. The moment he picked up the phone, he knew something was wrong.

"Antonia, what happened?" he asked, concern evident in his voice.

"Enzo just doesn't understand me," I sobbed. "He wants me to submit my work to a fashion magazine – but they won't appreciate it like an art publication would."

"Take a deep breath," Giovanni said gently. "Remember, you're the artist; your vision matters most. What do you think is best for your work?"

"An art magazine," I replied, sniffling. "But Enzo keeps saying that we need the exposure from the fashion world."

"Antonia, you deserve to have your work showcased where it will be truly appreciated," Giovanni reassured me. "Trust your instincts. If you believe that an art magazine is the right choice, stand your ground."

Giovanni's advice soothed me, and we continued talking late into the night. He reminded me of why I had fallen in love with surrealism in the first place – its ability to transport the viewer to another realm, to challenge their perceptions of reality. Our conversation rekindled my passion and determination.

The following week, Enzo invited a renowned gallery owner to our studio, hoping to secure a prestigious exhibition for my work. But as we entertained our guest, I couldn't help but feel uneasy. Enzo spent more time discussing himself and his photography than my paintings. It felt as if he was using my art as a stepping stone for his own career.

"Your work is remarkable, Antonia," the gallery owner said, sipping his wine. "But I must admit, I'm intrigued by Enzo's photography as well. Perhaps we could arrange a joint exhibition?"

"Absolutely," Enzo interjected enthusiastically before I could respond. "Our works complement each other perfectly."

I stared at him in disbelief. This was supposed to be about my art, not his ambitions. And it was then that I realized: my relationship with Enzo had become toxic. It was no longer about our shared passion for art but about his desire for fame and control.

"Excuse me," I muttered, feeling choked by the stifling atmosphere. I retreated to the bathroom, where I locked the door and allowed myself to cry. As the tears flowed, I knew deep down that something had to change. My love for Enzo was genuine, but so were his manipulations and selfishness. The time had come to reevaluate our relationship and decide whether it was worth the emotional turmoil.

I thought of Giovanni and how he always supported and encouraged my art without seeking anything in return. The contrast between him and Enzo was stark, and I couldn't ignore it any longer. My heart ached as I faced the reality of what needed to be done.

I stood in front of Enzo's apartment door, my heart pounding in my chest. The cold iron handle felt heavy as I hesitated, gripping it tightly. This was the moment I had been dreading but knew was necessary. Taking a deep breath, I pushed open the door and stepped inside.

"Antonia, my love," Enzo greeted me with his usual charm, a smile on his face and a glass of wine in hand. "What brings you here?"

"Enzo, we need to talk," I said, my voice trembled slightly, betraying my nerves.

"Ah, serious talks." He set down the wine glass and leaned against the wall, crossing his arms. "Go on then, what's on your mind?"

"Enzo... our relationship, it's not working for me anymore." My words hung heavily in the air like storm clouds ready to burst.

"Really? You're unhappy?" His eyebrows shot up in surprise, a hint of hurt flickering across his face. "Why, Antonia? Haven't I given you everything you wanted?"

"Everything I wanted?" I retorted, anger swelling within me. "You turned my art into a vehicle for your own ambitions. You've manipulated me and tried to control my career."

"Antonia, I only wanted what's best for us—"

"Best for us, or best for you?" I interrupted. "Giovanni has always supported me without asking for anything in return. He listens, he cares, and he doesn't try to steer my life in any direction other than where I want it to go. Can you say the same?"

"Is this about Giovanni?" Enzo scoffed, his eyes narrowing. "You're letting him come between us?"

"No, Enzo. This is about me and who I want to be," I replied firmly. "I can't keep sacrificing my happiness and my art for someone who doesn't truly value them."

"Antonia, please," he pleaded, reaching out for me. I recoiled, putting distance between us.

"Goodbye, Enzo." The words felt final as they left my lips. I turned away from him and walked out of the apartment, feeling both the weight of sadness and the lightness of relief.

As I stepped into the dimly lit street, tears blurred my vision. I had loved Enzo despite his flaws, but it was time to put myself first. My heart ached with regret, but I knew deep down that this was the right decision.

"Antonia?" Giovanni's concerned voice reached me as he walked towards me, having anticipated my need for support. He wrapped a comforting arm around my shoulders, and I leaned into his warmth. "Are you okay?"

"I will be, Giovanni," I whispered, knowing that with his steadfast friendship, I could begin healing and find my way back to what truly mattered: my passion for art and the freedom to create it on my own terms.

In the days that followed my breakup with Enzo, Giovanni was by my side. He knew when to offer words of encouragement and when to let silence speak volumes. We would walk through the city streets, taking in the sights and sounds that had always inspired me, but now felt even more vibrant and alive.

"Antonia," Giovanni said one afternoon as we sat at a small cafe, nursing warm cappuccinos, "it's time for you to channel your emotions into your art. You have so much talent and passion inside you – don't let it go to waste."

His words resonated with me, stirring something deep within my soul. I could feel the creative energy that had been dormant during my turbulent relationship with Enzo now bubbling to the surface. It was as if my heartache had opened a floodgate, allowing inspiration to pour forth.

"Maybe you're right," I agreed, my fingers itching to pick up a brush and translate my feelings onto canvas. "I need to focus on what truly matters to me."

Over the next few weeks, I threw myself into my work. My studio became a sanctuary, a place where I could lose myself in my paintings and forget the world outside. I painted like a woman possessed, each stroke of my brush an act of defiance against the constraints I had once allowed Enzo to impose upon me.

Giovanni encouraged me every step of the way, offering gentle critiques and praise in equal measure. As I worked, I found myself drawn to darker hues and more abstract forms, my art reflecting the turmoil and transformation I had experienced.

"Look at this, Giovanni," I said one day, stepping back from a particularly powerful piece, a whirlwind of colors and shapes that seemed to leap off the canvas. "This is what I needed to create. This is who I am."

"Antonia, it's magnificent," Giovanni replied, his eyes wide with admiration. "Your talent has always been evident, but now it's as if you're finally allowing yourself to soar."

"Thank you," I said softly, my heart swelling with gratitude for his unwavering support. "I couldn't have done this without you."

As I continued to delve deeper into my art, I began to find a sense of peace and healing that had long eluded me. My relationship with Enzo had left its scars, but with Giovanni by my side and my brush in hand, I knew I could face whatever the future held – strong, resilient, and free.

My days fell into a comforting rhythm, where the sun's gentle warmth and Giovanni's reassuring presence accompanied me. The bond between us grew stronger, as we spent more time together, sharing our thoughts on art, life, and everything in between.

"Antonia, have you ever considered trying a new medium?" Giovanni asked one day over a steaming cup of espresso at our favorite café. His eyes sparkled with curiosity and enthusiasm.

"Like what?" I replied, intrigued by his suggestion.

"Maybe sculpture? It could be an interesting way to explore your emotions and ideas in a more tactile form," he said, taking a sip of his coffee, his gaze unwavering.

"Perhaps," I mused, my mind already racing with possibilities. "I've never tried it before, but there's no harm in experimenting, right?"

"Exactly," Giovanni smiled, leaning back slightly in his chair, his fingers tapping rhythmically against the tabletop. "And I'll be right here to support you, every step of the way."

I couldn't help but smile at his steadfast encouragement. As the weeks passed, Giovanni and I found ourselves immersed in a new creative world, our hands covered in clay as we molded and shaped, giving life to our deepest emotions. It was fascinating to see how our art evolved side by side, each piece a reflection of our individual experiences and perspectives.

The connection between us only grew deeper, our conversations stretching late into the night as we shared our dreams and ambitions. Giovanni became not just a confidante but also a partner in my artistic journey, and I knew that his friendship was a rare and precious gift.

One evening, after a long day of sculpting, I stood back to admire my latest creation – a figure emerging from a swirling mass of darkness, reaching towards the light. It was raw, powerful, and undeniably mine.

"Look at this, Giovanni," I whispered, my voice filled with awe and pride. "I never thought I'd be able to create something like this."

"Antonia, it's incredible," he murmured, his eyes taking in every detail of the sculpture. "You've come so far, not just as an artist but as a person too."

I looked at him then, his face illuminated by the soft glow of the studio lights, and felt a surge of gratitude and affection. He had been there for me through the darkest of times, providing support and encouragement when I needed it the most.

"Thank you," I said, my voice barely audible over the sound of our breathing. "For everything."

He reached out and squeezed my hand gently, a silent acknowledgment of all that we had shared and overcome.

As I stood there, surrounded by the fruits of my labor and the warmth of Giovanni's friendship, I realized that I was no longer the same woman who had once been so ensnared by Enzo's charms. I had found my voice, my passion, and my purpose – and I was ready to embrace whatever life had in store for me, head held high and heart filled with determination.

CHAPTER 7

I stood in front of my easel, brush poised above the vibrant canvas. The smell of oil paints and turpentine filled my small studio, a scent that had become synonymous with my passion for art. I was Antonia Pageta, a young artist from a humble Italian village who dared to dream beyond the confines of tradition.

My strokes were bold and daring, reflecting the surrealistic style that had captivated me. The painting before me was a tribute to Spain, a visual representation of the turmoil that seemed to suffocate its very existence. The conflict between the Republicans and Franco's regime had left its mark not only on the hearts of the people but also on the physical environment that surrounded us.

"Antonia!" A voice called out from behind, snapping me back into reality. My hand slipped, leaving an unintended smear across the canvas. Frustration welled up inside me, but I knew better than to let it consume me. With a deep breath, I turned to face my visitor.

"Ah, Giovanni! What brings you here?"

He hesitated, his eyes darting between me and the painting. "Antonia, we cannot ignore what is happening outside these walls. The conflict between the Republicans and Franco's regime grows more dangerous each day. Innocent lives are being lost, and the world we know is crumbling."

His words weighed heavily on me, as I too had seen the destruction caused by the escalating war. The once picturesque landscapes in Spanish paintings that had inspired my early work were now marred by the detritus of battle and the scars of desolation. Images of grief-stricken families haunted my thoughts, but they also fueled my determination to fight for change.

67

"Giovanni, I understand your concern, but do not think for a moment that I am blind to the suffering around me. My art is a weapon, a powerful tool that can awaken the conscience of those who might be ignorant to the plight of our nation. Each stroke on this canvas is a testament to my love for the Spanish people and their land."

He stared at me, his expression a mixture of admiration and worry. "I know you believe in the power of art, Antonia, but I fear that it may not be enough. We must also take action, join forces with those who share our objectives."

"Perhaps you are right," I conceded, my gaze returning to my painting, the swirling colors now seeming to echo the chaos that engulfed us. "But for now, let me finish my work. Let me create something that will speak louder than any gun or bomb ever could."

As Giovanni left my studio, I couldn't shake the feeling that our lives were about to change irreversibly. Yet, despite the growing shadow of conflict that loomed over our country, I remained steadfast in my commitment to my artistic vision and my desire to fight for what I believed in. The brush in my hand felt like a sword, and with every stroke, I vowed to stand against the darkness that threatened to consume us all.

Weeks had passed since that fateful conversation with Giovanni, and the situation in Spain deteriorated rapidly. The streets were filled with fear, a palpable tension that seemed to hang heavy in the air like an oppressive fog. It was during these uncertain times that I made my decision - I would stand alongside the Republicans against Franco's regime. My art could not thrive under tyranny in Europe; I needed freedom and democracy to truly express myself.

"Antonia, you must be careful," whispered Giovanni one evening as we huddled together in my studio, the dim light casting shadows on his concerned face. "You are putting yourself at great risk."

"Freedom comes with a price, Giovanni," I replied, my voice resolute despite the tremor in my hands. "I am willing to pay it for the sake of my art and my people."

It was around this time that I heard mention of Lucia Moretti, a woman whose name was spoken with reverence among our fellow Republicans. They spoke of her courage, her unwavering dedication to fighting for justice and equality. In my heart, I knew I had to see this extraordinary woman.

Chance brought us together one cold evening, on the outskirts of a secret gathering of our comrades. As I approached the entrance, my steps faltering with nervous anticipation, I caught sight of a figure standing by a nearby tree. She was tall and imposing, her silhouette backlit by the faint glow of a cigarette. Her eyes met mine, and I saw in them a fierce determination that mirrored my own.

"Lucia Moretti?" I ventured, my voice barely audible above the howling wind.

"Si," she responded curtly, extinguishing her cigarette beneath the heel of her boot. "And you are Antonia Pageta, the artist?"

"Indeed, I am," I replied, feeling a surge of pride at being recognized by such a formidable woman. "I have heard much about you, and I believe our goals align."

"Then let us work together," she said, extending her hand to me in a gesture of solidarity. As I grasped her fingers, the strength of her grip sending a jolt through my arm, I knew that our alliance would be the catalyst for change - not only for the Spanish country but also for ourselves.

"Remember Antonia," Lucia said as we entered the gathering, her voice low and intense, "we fight not only for our freedom but also for the future generations who deserve to live in a just and equal society."

"Si," I whispered, my heart swelling with determination, "for them, and for our art."

-

The sun hung low in the sky, casting long shadows across the war-torn streets of Barcelona. The air was thick with tension as I made my way through the rubble, the smell of cordite a constant reminder of the conflict that raged around us. I couldn't help but feel a sense of unease prickling at the back of my neck, yet there was something else stirring within me - a burgeoning fire fueled by the desire to fight for my beliefs.

"Antonia Pageta?" A voice called out to me from behind a crumbling wall. I turned to find a woman with dark hair and piercing eyes watching me intently. She had a fierce, almost regal bearing, and her gaze seemed to cut straight through me, laying bare my very soul.

"Si," I replied cautiously, trying to keep my voice steady. "Lucia Moretti?"

"Indeed," she said with a slight nod, stepping out from behind the wall and into the fading sunlight. As we stood face to face, I felt the connection to this woman, who shared not only my passion for art but also my commitment to fighting for a better future for our country.

"Your paintings have inspired many of us," Lucia said, her words both thrilling and humbling me. "You have a powerful voice, Antonia, and it is one that must be heard."

"Thank you," I murmured, feeling a renewed sense of purpose as I realized the profound impact my art could have on others.

"However," Lucia continued, her tone growing more serious, "our work is far from over. We must continue to fight for justice and equality, to ensure that our voices are not silenced."

"Of course," I agreed, my resolve strengthening with each word she spoke. "But how do we proceed? How can I best use my art to further our cause?"

"By creating," Lucia replied firmly, her gaze never wavering from mine. "By using your talent to expose the brutality of this regime and give voice to those who have been silenced."

"Will you help me?" I asked, knowing that with her guidance and support, we could accomplish so much more together than we ever could alone.

"Si, Antonia," she said, a smile flickering across her lips as she extended her hand to me. "Together, we will fight for our art, our country, and our future."

As I clasped her hand in mine, feeling the warmth of her skin and the steadfast conviction in her grip, I knew that she was not only an ally but also a friend. Together, we would stand against the darkness and use our passion for art and justice to create a better world - one brushstroke at a time.

The sun was setting, casting an orange glow over the city streets as Lucia led me towards a dimly lit building. The sound of voices and laughter spilled through the open windows, and my fingers clenched around the handle of my artist's case as my heart raced in anticipation.

"Here," she said, pushing open the door to reveal a room filled with people huddled together in small groups, their voices fervent and animated. "This is where you can truly make a difference."

I hesitated on the threshold, feeling the weight of responsibility settle on my shoulders. As an artist, I had always believed that my work could change the world, but now, with Lucia by my side, I understood that my art alone would not be enough. I needed to join the fight against

Franco, to stand up for my beliefs and use my talent to advocate for human rights and democracy.

"Come," Lucia urged, her hand warm and reassuring on my arm. "Let us introduce ourselves to our new allies."

Together, we waded into the crowd, exchanging pleasantries and stories with the members of the local resistance group. As we spoke, I marveled at the diversity of people united by a common cause - farmers, teachers, artists like myself, all willing to risk their lives for the sake of freedom.

"Antonia," Lucia whispered, drawing me aside as a man began to address the group. "Remember, our shared goal is not only to fight against oppression but also to promote art and culture. Your work has the power to inspire, to give hope, to remind people of what we are fighting for."

Her words resonated within me, igniting a fire of determination that burned away my lingering doubts and fears. As I listened to the impassioned speeches of my fellow fighters, their words interwoven with images of suffering and injustice, I knew that I had found my purpose.

When the meeting finally drew to a close, I approached Lucia with a newfound sense of resolve. "I want to create a mural," I told her, my voice steady and confident. "A work of art that will symbolize our struggle and the importance of human rights."

"Si, Antonia," she agreed, her eyes shining with pride. "Together, we will create something truly powerful, a testament to the indomitable spirit of our people."

As we left the building arm in arm, our footsteps echoing against the cobblestone streets, I knew that our journey was just beginning. Together, Lucia and I would use our talents and our passion for justice to make a difference, one brushstroke at a time. And as we walked towards the fading light of the setting sun, I felt a renewed sense of hope - for our art, our beliefs, and our future.

The acrid scent of paint mingled with the ever-present haze of dust and smoke in the air, creating a bittersweet symphony of art and war. As my brush traced bold strokes of color across the crumbling wall, I felt Lucia's eyes upon me, watching my every move with keen interest. My heart raced, not only from the thrill of our clandestine act but also from the unspoken bond that continued to grow between us.

"Antonia," she whispered, her voice barely audible above the distant rumble of gunfire. "You have such a gift. I can see your soul in every line you draw."

"Gracias," I murmured, my cheeks flushing with both embarrassment and pride. The weight of her words humbled me, filling me with a renewed sense of purpose. We were creating something meaningful, something that would endure long after the last echoes of battle had faded away.

"Quietly now, we must be careful no one sees us," Lucia urged, glancing nervously over her shoulder. Though we had chosen an isolated spot for our mural, the looming threat of discovery was ever-present. Our defiance of Franco's regime was dangerous, and both of us knew the consequences of being caught.

As we worked side by side, our brushes weaving a tapestry of hope and resistance, I found myself opening up to Lucia in ways I never thought possible. We shared stories of loss and pain, of dreams shattered and rebuilt anew. In her, I found a kindred spirit - someone who understood my need to fight, to create, to make a difference in this world.

"Once, my father told me that our family's blood runs thick with passion and rebellion," Lucia confided, her eyes distant as she recalled her childhood. "He said it was both a blessing and a curse, for we are destined to stand against tyranny, even at the cost of our own lives."

"Your father was a wise man," I replied softly, my heart aching for her loss. "And his legacy lives on through you."

"Through both of us," she corrected gently, her gaze meeting mine with the fierce determination that had first drawn me to her.

The days that followed were a blur of exhilaration and terror. We continued our work on the mural, stealing night after night from the sleep we so desperately needed. Our bodies grew weary, but our spirits remained unbroken, fueled by the knowledge that our art would serve as a beacon of hope for those who still suffered under Franco's rule.

But our defiance did not go unnoticed. The whispers of discontent grew louder, the shadows that lurked at the edges of our vision more sinister. One by one, our fellow resistance members vanished, their fates unknown but all too easily imagined.

"Antonia, we must be careful," Lucia warned, a tremor of fear in her voice. "They are watching us. We cannot let our passion blind us to the dangers we face."

"Si, Lucia," I agreed solemnly. "We will finish our mural, and then we must find another way to fight. For our art, our beliefs, and our future."

As we put the final touches on our masterpiece, our fingers stained with paint and sweat, I felt a surge of pride unlike anything I had ever experienced before. We had created something beautiful, something powerful - a testament to the indomitable spirit of our people. And though the road ahead was uncertain, I knew that together, Lucia and I would continue to make a difference, one brushstroke at a time.

Days turned into weeks, and the dangers we faced grew more apparent with each passing moment. Lucia and I knew that we had to keep fighting for our art and our beliefs, but we also recognized the need for a new approach. We could no longer rely solely on painting murals or speaking out at crowded meetings; we needed to find fresh ways to spread our message and resist Franco's regime.

"Antonia," Lucia whispered one evening as we sat huddled together in a dimly lit corner of a local café, our heads bent over a tattered map of the city. "I have an idea."

"Tell me," I replied, my fingers tracing the streets of our beloved city, imagining the places where our next act of defiance could take place.

Lucia leaned in closer, her warm breath tickling my ear. "We attend the upcoming rally, but not just as spectators. We create art right there, on the spot—something so powerful, so bold, that it cannot be ignored."

My heart raced at the thought, equal parts excitement and trepidation coursing through my veins. "It will be dangerous, Lucia. They will surely be watching."

"Of course, it is dangerous," she responded, her eyes flashing with determination. "But we cannot let fear dictate our actions, Antonia. Our art is our weapon, and we must use it to fight for what we believe in."

I nodded, knowing that she was right. We were artists, after all, and the power of our creations spoke louder than any words ever could. If we wanted to make a difference, we needed to embrace the risks and face them head-on.

"Alright," I agreed, my voice filled with resolve. "We'll do it. We'll create something unforgettable at the rally, something that will inspire hope and spark change."

Lucia smiled, her hand clasping mine in a gesture of solidarity. "Together, Antonia. We will do this together."

And so, as the day of the rally approached, Lucia and I spent countless hours preparing for our audacious act of resistance. We gathered supplies, sketched out ideas, and practiced techniques that would enable us to create our masterpiece quickly and efficiently while evading the watchful eyes of Franco's forces.

The morning of the rally dawned bright and clear, a perfect backdrop for our daring endeavor. As we made our way through the throngs of people, I could feel the energy in the air – a palpable sense of anticipation that both frightened and exhilarated me.

"Ready, Antonia?" Lucia asked, her hand resting on my shoulder as we stood at the edge of the crowd.

"Si," I replied, my heart pounding in my chest. "Let's show them what we're made of."

With a nod, we stepped forward, our brushes poised and ready, our spirits united by a shared commitment to fight for our art, our beliefs, and our future. No matter the dangers that lay ahead, we knew that our cause was worth every risk. And as we began our latest creation, I couldn't help but think: This is only the beginning. Together, Lucia and I will continue to make a difference, one brushstroke at a time.

CHAPTER 8

The year was 1938, and Europe stood on the precipice of disaster. As an artist, I could feel the dark clouds looming over us all, casting their shadows across the once-bustling streets of Barcelona. My name is Antonia Pageta, a 25-year-old abstract artist who had long dreamt of leaving an indelible mark on the world through my creations. But as a Jewish woman in Franco, Hitler and Mussolini's reign of terror, I knew that this would be no ordinary path to carve.

"Antonia, you must keep creating," I whispered to myself one morning, my hands stained with paint, my spirit weighed down by what seemed like an insurmountable challenge. "Do not let them take this from you."

I had been born with fire in my blood, the kind that ignited my heart and soul whenever I picked up a paintbrush. My abstract art represented so much more than simple shapes and colors — it was the manifestation of my deepest emotions and desires. And yet, as a Jewish woman in the oppressive regime, I knew my very existence was under threat.

"Frau Pageta," Hans, an art dealer, said to me one day, his eyes cold and unfeeling. "Your work is powerful, but I am afraid we cannot represent your art." The heavy silence that followed felt like a punch to the gut. I knew that it wasn't just about the art; it was about my heritage and my gender.

"Is it because I'm Jewish?" I asked him, my voice barely above a whisper. "Or is it because I am a woman?"

"Both," he answered bluntly. "The world has changed, Antonia. You are a talented artist, but there is no room for your kind in our galleries anymore."

As I walked away from that meeting, my heart shattered into a million pieces. I had always believed that my art could transcend the barriers of race and gender, that it would be judged solely on its merit. But now, I was forced to confront the fact that I had been naïve. My Jewish heritage and my identity as a woman made me a target for persecution and rejection in a world that seemed hell-bent on extinguishing any semblance of beauty or truth.

"Perhaps it's time to leave Barcelona," I whispered to myself one cold night as I stared out at the empty streets, my heart heavy with sorrow. "Perhaps it's time to find a place where I can create without fear."

And so, in the midst of chaos and uncertainty, I resolved to fight for my dreams – even if it meant leaving behind everything I had ever known. For in the end, there was only one thing I could cling to: my unwavering belief in the power of art to heal, inspire, and unite us all.

I could feel the menacing gaze of passersby on my back as I packed my belongings in haste. A sense of urgency gnawed at me; time was running out. The oppressive regime had cast its dark shadow over Europe, and the streets now whispered with fear.

"Antonia, you must leave as soon as possible," my dear friend Elise had warned me. "Your Jewish heritage puts you in grave danger here."

I knew she was right. With each passing day, the air grew heavier with a suffocating weight. I found myself looking over my shoulder, my heart pounding in my chest. And so, in the dead of night, I slipped away from Barcelona, leaving behind the city that had once welcomed me with open arms.

My journey took me back to Paris, a city known for its art and culture – a sanctuary where I hoped to find refuge. Upon arrival, I sought out the Mythic Kunst, a group of artists who prided themselves on their avant-garde approach to creativity. Little did I know the bitter truth that awaited me.

"Sorry, Antonia," said one of the artists, a man named Henri, as he examined my portfolio. "We cannot accept you into our community."

"May I ask why?" I inquired, my voice trembling with disappointment and disbelief.

"Your abstract style is interesting, but we cannot ignore your Jewish heritage," he replied, his voice devoid of empathy. "It would put us all at risk should we associate with you."

"Is my art not enough to speak for itself?" I demanded, anger and frustration boiling inside me. "Why should my identity as a Jewish woman artist matter?"

"Things have changed, Antonia," another artist chimed in solemnly. "These are dangerous times for everyone, especially for people like you. We must protect ourselves."

Feeling the sting of rejection, I turned away from them, fighting back the tears that threatened to spill. Paris, I realized, was not the haven I had imagined it to be. Even in this city of light, the dark cloud of prejudice and hatred loomed large.

"Perhaps there is nowhere safe for me," I whispered to myself as I walked along the Seine, watching the murky water flow beneath the bridges. "Maybe my only choice is to hide who I am and abandon my art."

But deep down, something inside me rebelled against that thought. I couldn't imagine a life without my art – it was the very essence of my soul, a beacon of hope in even the darkest of times.

"Never give up, Antonia," I murmured, clutching my portfolio tightly to my chest. "You must keep creating, no matter what."

I knew then that I would have to forge my own path, carving out a place for myself in a world that seemed determined to reject me. And with every brushstroke, every splash of color on canvas, I would continue to challenge the oppressive forces that sought to tear me apart. For I was an artist, and nothing could extinguish the fire that burned within me.

As I wandered the streets of Paris, my heart ached with the knowledge that I had been cast out by the very people I had hoped would embrace me. The biting wind seemed to echo my loneliness as it whipped through the narrow alleys, and it was all too easy to imagine the Mythic Kunst laughing at me behind closed doors. "How naïve, how foolish I was," I thought bitterly, hugging my coat tighter around me.

"Excusez-moi, Mademoiselle, are you lost?" A kind voice interrupted my dark musings. I looked up to see a middle-aged man with a warm smile, his eyes filled with genuine concern.

"No, Merci, Monsieur," I replied, forcing a half-hearted smile. "Just trying to find my way."

"Ah, Paris can be overwhelming at times," he nodded understandingly. "If you don't mind me asking, what brings you here?"

I hesitated, unsure if I should reveal the truth. But something about this stranger's kindness compelled me to open up. "I am an artist, seeking refuge from the darkness that is engulfing Europe. But even here, I find myself rejected because of who I am and the art I create."

"Artists must stick together in these difficult times," he said gently, placing a comforting hand on my shoulder. "There is a small community of artists that meet near Montmartre. They may not have the prestige of the Mythic Kunst, but they understand the importance of supporting one another. Perhaps you could find solace among them?"

"Thank you, Monsieur," I whispered gratefully, tears welling up in my eyes. "I will try."

"Bon courage, Mademoiselle," he smiled, before continuing on his way.

I spent the following days searching for this haven, this community of fellow artists who might be willing to embrace me and my work. As I explored the winding streets of Montmartre, I discovered a world of bohemian cafes, art studios, and colorful characters who defied the conventions of the time.

"Excusez-moi," I approached a group of painters in one such café, their palettes brimming with vibrant hues. "I was told there is a community of artists here who support one another. Might I join you?"

"Ah, bien sûr!" one of the artists exclaimed, extending an invitation to sit with them. "We are always eager to welcome new members. Come, share your ideas with us."

"Finally," I thought, as I met these kindred spirits, my heart swelling with hope.

To survive in Paris, I needed to find work. My artistic endeavors alone would not pay the bills and I couldn't return to Enzo's world of modelling. I found employment at a small café near my newfound circle of friends. The job was tiring, but it allowed me to keep a roof over my head and continue pursuing my art.

"Bonjour, Madame," I greeted my first customer of the day, balancing a tray laden with steaming cups of coffee. "Un café noir, s'il vous plaît," she replied, her eyes scanning the headlines of Le Monde.

"Antonia, don't forget to smile," my boss chided me gently as he passed by. I forced a grin upon my face and refocused on my tasks.

"Oui, Monsieur," I sighed inwardly, feeling the weight of the past few months settling on my shoulders. My life had changed beyond recognition, and yet, I clung to the belief that art could still offer me solace.

Despite the challenges, I pressed forward, determined to rebuild my life in this city of light and shadow. My new artist friends offered me a sense of belonging and purpose, and their encouragement fueled my creativity. I would not let the Mythic Kunst, or anyone else, define my worth as an artist. I would rise above their rejection and prove to myself that I could still create magic with my brushstrokes.

I stood before the large canvas, my hands trembling and my heart pounding as I dipped the brush into the vibrant blue paint. My thoughts raced, riddled with questions and doubts. Was there any place for me in this male-dominated art world? Confronted by constant rejection, I felt like an imposter.

"Antonia, you need to push through," whispered my fellow artist friend, Marcel, as he approached me. "You cannot let their narrow-mindedness stop you from creating."

"Push through?" I scoffed, frustration bubbling up within me. "I am a woman, and a Jew at that. It feels as though no matter how hard I work, the doors will remain closed to me."

"Have faith in yourself," Marcel insisted. "Your talent is undeniable, but you must fight for your place, just as we all do."

"Fight? Is that what this is? A never-ending battle against the prejudices and ignorance of others?" My voice was strained, cracking under the weight of my emotions.

"Unfortunately, yes," Marcel admitted, his eyes filled with sympathy. "But remember, Antonia, you are not alone. We stand with you, united in our quest for artistic freedom."

"Thank you, Marcel." I sighed, feeling a small flicker of hope reignite in my chest. "But sometimes, it feels as if my heritage only serves to make me more vulnerable in this tumultuous time. I fear for my safety and my future."

"Your fears are justified, but you cannot let them paralyze you," Marcel urged. "Continue to create, continue to defy those who would silence your distinctive voice."

"Perhaps you're right," I conceded, forcing myself to breathe deeply and steady my hand. "I'll keep fighting, for my art and for my life."

"Good," Marcel smiled encouragingly. "Now, let's see what magic you can create with that brush."

As I returned my focus to the canvas, my resolve strengthened. I would not let the Mythic Kunst or the male-dominated art world define me, nor would I allow fear to dictate my life. With each stroke of the brush, I would defy those who sought to silence and oppress me; I would fight for my place in this world.

"Watch me," I whispered, determination etched across my features as I swept vibrant colors onto the canvas. "Watch me soar."

The streets of Paris were alive with the sounds of laughter, music, and the clatter of horse-drawn carriages. I walked through the bustling crowd, feeling the cobblestone beneath my worn-out shoes, and tugged at the collar of my coat to protect myself from the chilly air. The weight of my sketchbook pressed against my side, a reminder of the art that once consumed me, now a hollow echo of the past.

The scent of fresh bread and strong coffee wafted through the air as I approached the small café where I worked. My boss, Monsieur Lefèvre, greeted me with his usual gruff demeanor. "You're late again, Antonia. Get to work."

"Sorry, Monsieur," I mumbled, quickly tying on my apron. As I weaved through the tables taking orders, the conversations around me bubbled like a cacophony of discordant notes.

Snippets of talk about politics and war filtered into my consciousness, making my heart race with anxiety.

"Your hands are trembling," whispered Claire, a fellow waitress and friend, as I poured her a cup of coffee in the back room. "Is everything all right?"

"Sometimes it feels like I'm standing at the edge of a cliff," I confessed, staring into the dark liquid, "and I'm not sure if I should jump or stay put."

"Antonia, your art is extraordinary. You mustn't let the opinions of these narrow-minded fools define you," she said, placing a comforting hand on my arm. "But I understand why you're scared. It's not easy being a Jewish woman in this world, especially now."

"Exactly," I sighed. "Not only do I feel rejected by the very people I thought would embrace my work, but every day I fear for my safety. I don't know if I can continue living like this."

"Then perhaps it's time for a change," Claire suggested, her voice gentle yet firm. "Sometimes, we must forge our own path, away from those who would hold us back."

I looked out the window at the vibrant Parisian streets, my heart aching with yearning and uncertainty. Could I truly leave everything behind - my art, my friends, and the life I once knew? Was there a place for me in this chaotic world, where I could be accepted as both an artist and a Jewish woman?

"Maybe you're right," I whispered, my resolve beginning to crystalize like frost on the glass pane. "Maybe it's time for me to find my own way."

"Whatever you decide, Antonia, know that I'll support you," Claire said, squeezing my hand before returning to the busy café floor.

As I turned away from the window, I felt the familiar weight of my sketchbook against my side, its blank pages waiting to be filled with color and life. I knew then that the only way to confront my fears and reclaim my identity was to create art that defied the constraints placed upon me. I would not let this turning point defeat me; I would embrace it, and use it to fuel my passion.

"Watch me," I murmured, determination surging through my veins. "Watch me rise above."

Days turned into weeks as the Parisian autumn chill settled over the city. The once vibrant leaves of the trees lining the boulevards now lay scattered across the cobblestones, trampled underfoot by the bustling crowds who paid them no heed. I found myself wandering these streets with an uneasy heart, searching for a place where I could belong.

"Is my art worth anything?" I asked myself, staring at a blank canvas in a dusty corner of my small apartment. "And if what defines me is my art, what does that make me?"

I sought solace in my work at the café, immersing myself in the scents of freshly baked pastries and strong coffee, the sounds of lively conversation and laughter. But as I navigated the cramped spaces between the tables, balancing trays laden with steaming cups and warm plates, I couldn't escape the gnawing feeling that I was living a lie.

"Antonia, you should try to meet some new people," Claire suggested one evening as we shared a simple meal by the window. "There are other artists out there who don't care about your heritage or gender. You just need to find them."

"Perhaps," I replied, picking at my food with little appetite. "But it's difficult to trust anyone when the world has become so hostile."

"True, but you can't hide forever. We must adapt and grow, even in darkness," she insisted, her eyes filled with determination.

Her words echoed in my mind as I walked through the lamp-lit streets, their shadows casting eerie patterns on the ancient stone walls. I began to frequent underground gatherings, where artists of all kinds gathered to share their work. But each time I revealed my identity, I was met with suspicion and mistrust. It seemed that even among those who claimed to defy convention, prejudices still ran deep.

"Maybe this is the end," I thought, a wave of despair washing over me as I returned to my empty apartment one night. "Maybe there's no place for me in this world."

"Antonia, you mustn't lose hope," Claire's voice whispered in my memory. "Remember who you are - a talented artist with a unique vision. Don't let them take that away from you."

I realized then that the only way to find my place in the world was to create it myself, even if it meant facing rejection and persecution. The thought both terrified and exhilarated me, but as I gazed out at the city skyline, I knew I had no choice.

"From now on, I will forge my own path," I vowed, feeling the weight of uncertainty heavy on my shoulders. "And whatever lies ahead, I'll face it head-on - as Antonia Pageta, Italian, Jewish woman and artist."

As I stood there, staring into the unknown future, I couldn't help but wonder what challenges awaited me, and if I would be strong enough to overcome them. And though I felt small and alone in the vast, unforgiving city, I also felt a spark of defiance beginning to burn within me, urging me onward.

CHAPTER 9

The sun dipped low in the sky, casting a golden hue over the bustling streets of Paris. I strode purposefully toward my small rented studio, my sketchbook clutched tightly to my chest. I'd found solace in my work, channeling my newfound determination into each brushstroke.

"Ah, Antonia!" called out Massimo, a fellow artist who shared the same building as my studio. His warm smile greeted me as I approached. "Working late again?"

"Of course," I replied with a grin, feeling a sense of camaraderie with him that had only grown since I'd started asserting myself. "My inspiration cannot be tamed by the setting sun."

"Nor should it be," he chuckled, clapping me on the shoulder. "I've noticed a change in you, Antonia. Your art has always been extraordinary, but now there's a fire behind your eyes that wasn't there before."

"Thank you, Massimo," I said, touched by his observation. "I've learned that I must stand up for my beliefs and take risks to grow as an artist."

"Bravo," he nodded approvingly. "May we all learn from your example."

As I entered my studio, I marveled at how much my relationships had evolved since I'd embraced my authentic self. No longer did I feel overshadowed or intimidated by my colleagues; instead, I saw them as allies, sharing the same passion for artistic expression. My connections with friends had deepened too, as they recognized and respected my renewed commitment to my craft.

In the days that followed, I embraced challenges I once would have shied away from. A prestigious gallery owner visited our shared studio space and, rather than retreating to the shadows as I might have done before, I boldly introduced myself and presented my work. The owner was so impressed that he offered me a solo exhibition—a dream I'd scarcely dared to imagine.

"Antonia, you did it!" Massimo exclaimed as we celebrated my upcoming exhibition with our fellow artists. "You took control of your destiny, and look where it's led you!"

"Indeed," I mused, raising my glass in a toast. "To following our dreams, no matter the obstacles we face."

"Here, here!" they chorused, their voices filling the room with joyous laughter.

As I stood among them, surrounded by their warmth and support, I knew I'd found not only my voice but also my true self. With each step forward, I embraced the journey of personal growth, knowing it would forever shape my art and my life.

It was a chilly autumn evening as I sat in my studio, staring at the blank canvas before me. The air was crisp with the scent of oil paints and turpentine, a comforting reminder of my endless pursuit of artistic expression. As the sun dipped below the horizon, casting a warm glow across the room, I couldn't help but feel a sudden pang of doubt.

"Antonia, what's bothering you?" Sofia asked gently, stepping into the studio with her usual grace. Her eyes searched mine, clearly able to see past the façade I'd constructed.

"I've been struggling lately," I admitted, brushing a stray lock of hair from my forehead. "Ever since that gallery owner visited our shared space, I can't seem to find the inspiration I once had. It feels like there's a wall between me and my creativity."

Sofia's gaze softened, and she moved to sit beside me on the stool. "You've grown so much, Antonia," she murmured, placing a hand on my shoulder. "But growth can be painful, too. Remember when you first began to assert yourself among your colleagues, or when you pursued opportunities that once terrified you? You overcame those challenges and emerged stronger for it."

I sighed, recalling the moments when my newfound confidence had propelled me forward. "You're right, Sofia," I conceded. "But this feels different, somehow. What if I can't overcome this obstacle?"

"Everyone faces setbacks, Antonia," she replied, her voice firm yet compassionate. "The important thing is how you respond to them. Take this as an opportunity to grow even more—to push beyond your current boundaries and discover new depths within yourself."

As I absorbed her words, I felt a spark of determination ignite within me. She was right—adversity was a part of life, and I could choose to let it defeat me or use it as a catalyst for further growth.

"Thank you, Sofia," I whispered, my voice heavy with gratitude. "I will use this setback as a chance to evolve and strengthen my resolve."

With renewed vigor, I approached the canvas once more. As I dipped my brush into the vibrant colors, I no longer saw the blank space as a symbol of my inadequacy but instead as an opportunity to create something new and profound.

"Remember, Antonia," Sofia called softly as she left the room, "the greatest masterpieces are often born from the most difficult struggles."

And so, with each stroke of the brush, I poured my heart and soul into the canvas. I embraced the adversity that had threatened to consume me, transforming it into a breathtaking work of art that stood as a testament to the power of perseverance and personal growth.

Months had passed since that fateful conversation with Sofia, and the impact of her words still resonated within me. Each day, I felt myself becoming more attuned to my art and the world around me, as though some hidden veil had been lifted from my eyes. The gradual metamorphosis was subtle yet undeniable; I could feel its effects in every aspect of my life.

"Antonia!" a cheerful voice called from behind me as I stood in front of my easel, immersed in my latest creation. I turned to see my dear friend and fellow artist, Giovanni, entering my studio with his usual exuberance.

"Giovanni," I greeted him warmly, noticing how my tone had become richer, more self-assured since our first meeting. "What brings you here?"

"Ah, just wanted to see your latest masterpiece," he replied, his eyes dancing with excitement as he approached the canvas. "I've heard whispers of your incredible new work."

As I watched Giovanni study the painting, I thought back to my earlier days when I would have wilted under such scrutiny. But now, something had shifted inside me. I stood tall, shoulders squared, and met his gaze without flinching. I knew this piece was a true reflection of my soul, and I was proud to share it with the world.

"Antonia," he finally spoke, admiration evident in his voice, "this is... astounding. The depth, the emotion—it's breathtaking."

"Thank you," I whispered, feeling a warm glow spread through me at his praise. I had come so far since those dark days of self-doubt and defeat, each step on my path toward personal growth leaving me stronger, more capable than before.

"Your technique has improved considerably," he observed, tracing the intricate patterns of color on the canvas. "You've really taken Sofia's advice to heart, haven't you?"

I nodded, a small smile playing at the corners of my lips. "She taught me that every obstacle we face is an opportunity for growth. It's up to us to seize it and allow ourselves to be transformed."

"Indeed," he agreed, his eyes still locked on the painting. "And you, my friend, have certainly done just that."

As I stood there, basking in the warmth of his admiration, I realized just how far I had come on this journey of personal growth. The once timid and uncertain girl from the village was now a confident and self-assured woman, unafraid to face the world and all its challenges head-on.

"Thank you, Giovanni," I murmured, returning my gaze to the canvas. "And now, if you'll excuse me, I have a masterpiece to finish."

With renewed determination, I picked up my brush and began to paint once more, each stroke a testament to the power of perseverance and the incredible transformation it had wrought within me.

As I stood in my sunlit studio, the soft murmurs of conversation and clinking wine glasses drifted through the air from the gallery beyond. My latest exhibition was well underway, attended by friends, fellow artists, and curious passersby alike. I watched as they studied each piece with furrowed brows and thoughtful nods, their quiet contemplation punctuated by the occasional gasp of surprise or whispered praise.

"Brava, Antonia!" Sofia exclaimed, sweeping into the studio with a warm embrace, her eyes alight with pride. "Your work has never been more stunning."

"Thank you," I replied, my cheeks flushed with both gratitude and humility. As I looked around at the gathered crowd, it dawned on me that my art - once merely an outlet for my own emotions and dreams - now resonated with others, inspiring them to see the world through my unique lens.

"Antonia, your work has truly evolved," said Carla, a fellow artist whose opinion I respected greatly. "It's amazing how much you've grown."

"Indeed," I mused, recalling the countless hours spent honing my craft, learning from my mistakes, and pushing past self-doubt. "And I couldn't have done it without the support of everyone here."

"Nor could we have grown without your inspiration," Sofia countered, her hand resting warmly on my shoulder. "You've shown us all the power of perseverance and staying true to ourselves."

"Here's to you, Antonia," Carla chimed in, raising her glass in a toast. "To your growth, your art, and your ever-burning passion."

"Cheers!" the others echoed, their voices swelling with warmth and admiration.

As I raised my own glass in celebration, I marveled at the realization that my personal journey of growth had not only changed me but also those around me. No longer bound by fear and uncertainty, my newfound confidence had become a beacon of hope and inspiration for others.

"Thank you," I whispered into the jubilant chorus, my heart swelling with gratitude. "This is only the beginning."

And as I gazed upon my creations - each one a testament to the trials and triumphs of my personal journey - I knew that there would be many more milestones to come, each one marking another step on the path toward artistic mastery and self-discovery.

"Let's create together," I said to Sofia and Carla, my eyes sparkling with renewed determination. "Let's all continue to grow, and show the world what we're capable of."

"Agreed," they chorused, and with that, we turned our attention back to the exhibition, emboldened by the knowledge that when we embraced our personal growth, anything was possible.

CHAPTER 10

The sun dipped below the horizon, casting a warm golden hue over my studio. I stood back to admire my latest masterpiece – an abstract swirl of dancers with vibrant colors that seemed to move across the canvas in a wild tango of emotion. My name is Antonia Pageta, and I am a successful artist whose work has gained recognition in the art world for its unique style.

"Antonia, you've truly outdone yourself this time!" my agent, Carlotta, exclaimed as she examined the painting with her expert eye. We had worked together for years, and she had always been a firm believer in my talent.

"Thank you, Carlotta," I replied, a small smile playing on my lips. "But, I'm afraid this might be my last piece."

"Last piece?" she echoed, her face a mask of shock and confusion. "What do you mean?"

I sighed, feeling the weight of my decision settle heavily upon my shoulders. Despite my success and recognition, I couldn't shake the nagging feeling that the art world did not truly appreciate or understand my work. Instead of celebrating my unique vision, they were content to box me into categories that didn't fit, to label me as something safe and palatable. It was suffocating, and I could no longer bear it.

"Carlotta, I've decided to renounce creating art altogether," I said with finality, bracing myself for her reaction.

"Antonia, you can't be serious!" she protested, her eyes wide with disbelief. "You're at the height of your career! The world needs your art!"

"Does it, though?" I questioned, my voice heavy with doubt. "Or does it just need another commodity to sell? Another name to drop at cocktail parties?"

"Antonia, don't let the cynicism of the art world get to you," Carlotta pleaded. "Your work is important, and there are people who genuinely appreciate it."

"Perhaps," I conceded. "But that's not enough for me anymore. I need to step away from the noise, the pressure — rediscover the passion that once drove me."

"Antonia, think about this carefully," she implored. "You've worked so hard to get where you are today. Are you truly willing to walk away from everything?"

I thought back to my humble beginnings in a small Italian village, my unwavering commitment to my artistic vision, and the fierce determination that had brought me this far. Yes, I had achieved much — but at what cost? My love for art was waning, replaced by disillusionment with an industry that cared more for profit than true expression.

"Carlotta, I have thought about it," I said quietly. "And I know that I can't continue down this path any longer. I have to find a different way."

As I spoke those words, I felt a strange sense of relief wash over me. For the first time in years, I allowed myself to imagine a life outside the confines of the art world — a life where my creativity would no longer be stifled, and where I could once again find joy in my work. And though I knew the road ahead would be challenging, I couldn't help but feel a spark of excitement at the prospect of a new beginning.

The art world had betrayed me. They praised my work, then suffocated my creativity beneath their expectations and greed. My passion for the brush and canvas had been smothered, replaced by a hollow longing to escape. The more I achieved, the more they demanded of me; the more I painted, the less it felt like my own. And then the same people who had praised my work began to insult me for being a Jew. I needed to flee Paris, and France, and find safety in another country.

I decided to withdraw from the world that had once admired me, seeking solace in the one place where I could truly be free: nature. I recalled the simple beauty of the English countryside from the work of the Romantic artists, and my heart yearned to go there. And so, with a heavy but determined heart, I packed my belongings and embarked on a journey to the Lake District in England – a place where I hoped to rediscover myself.

As I stepped out of the train at the small village station, a wave of calm washed over me. I could feel my soul begin to heal as I breathed in the crisp, clean air. It was a far cry from the heat of Italy or the stifling metropolis I had left behind: no more blinking neon lights or honking car horns, just the gentle rustle of leaves and the distant sound of sheep grazing.

"Miss Pageta?" A soft voice called out to me, and I turned to see an elderly man with a warm smile. "I'm Mr. Thompson, your landlord. Welcome to our little corner of paradise."

"Thank you," I replied, shaking his hand. "It's even more beautiful than I remembered."

Mr. Thompson led me down a narrow path lined with wildflowers, past quaint stone houses and gently rolling hills, until we reached my new home: a charming, ivy-covered cottage tucked away amidst lush greenery. As he handed me the keys, I knew I had made the right decision.

"Enjoy your stay, Miss Pageta," he said kindly. "And remember, if you need anything, don't hesitate to ask."

"Thank you, Mr. Thompson," I replied, my heart swelling with gratitude. "I think I have everything I need right here."

As I settled into my new life in the village, I embraced the quiet simplicity that surrounded me. I spent my days reading by the fireplace, listening to birdsong, and wandering through the serene woods, feeling the earth beneath my feet and losing myself in the beauty of the landscape.

In this peaceful haven, far removed from the suffocating grip of the art world, I allowed my mind to wander and my creativity to flow once more. The spark that had been extinguished within me began to flicker back to life, ignited by the tranquility of my surroundings and the freedom of my solitude. And as I gazed out across the verdant fields, I felt a renewed sense of purpose take root within my soul – a purpose that would guide me on my journey back to the canvas, and lead me to create again.

The first few weeks in my new surroundings were more challenging than I had anticipated. My cottage, though charming and filled with character, lacked the modern amenities I had grown accustomed to in the city. Washing clothes by hand in a small basin and cooking over an open fire seemed like a romantic notion at first, but soon the novelty wore off, and I longed for the convenience of my old life.

"Antonia, why are you doing this to yourself?" I muttered as I struggled to light the fire once again. The damp wood refused to catch, and my fingers grew numb from the cold. Frustration welled up inside me, threatening to boil over.

"Ah, Miss Pageta," Mr. Thompson called out one afternoon as I passed his house on my way to the local market. "How are you finding village life?"

"Quite different from what I'm used to, Mr. Thompson," I admitted, trying to sound cheerful. "But change is good, isn't it?"

"Indeed, it is," he agreed, nodding sagely. "And speaking of change, have you had a chance to explore the village yet? It's rather quaint, but there's quite a bit to see."

"Actually, I haven't," I confessed. "I've been too busy settling in."

"Perhaps tomorrow morning, I could show you around," he suggested kindly. "There's a lovely little market just down the road, and a beautiful lake nearby."

"Thank you, Mr. Thompson. I'd like that very much."

As promised, the next day Mr. Thompson led me through the narrow cobblestone streets of the village. The houses were a delightful mix of stone and timber-framed structures with thatched roofs, their aged facades softened by tangles of ivy and fragrant climbing roses. We stopped at the bustling market square, where villagers bartered for fresh produce, locally made cheeses, and handcrafted wares. The air was filled with the sounds of laughter and lively conversation, a stark contrast to the hushed silence that enveloped my cottage.

"Over there is the village bakery," Mr. Thompson pointed out. "Their scones are simply divine. And just beyond, you'll find the butcher and the grocer."

"Thank you for showing me around, Mr. Thompson," I said gratefully. "It's nice to see there's still some semblance of community here."

"Of course, Miss Pageta," he replied with a warm smile. "We may be a small village, but we look out for one another."

As we continued our tour, we approached the nearby lake, its glassy surface reflecting the dappled sunlight that filtered through the trees. A gentle breeze ruffled the water, creating delicate ripples that danced across its depths.

"Isn't it lovely?" Mr. Thompson asked, his eyes sparkling as he gazed at the serene scene before us. "I often come here to think or just enjoy the peace and quiet."

"Indeed," I murmured, captivated by the beauty of the landscape. "It's truly inspiring."

"Ah, yes," he agreed, his expression turning thoughtful. "I can only imagine what an artist like yourself might create after spending some time here."

His words struck a chord deep within me. As much as I had tried to leave my artistic life behind, the allure of this enchanting village began to awaken something inside me. The vibrant colors of the market, the rich textures of the ancient buildings, and the mesmerizing tranquility of the lake stirred a familiar longing in my heart – a yearning to capture the essence of this place on canvas.

"Perhaps one day, Mr. Thompson," I said softly, a faint smile playing on my lips. "Perhaps one day."

My days began to take on a certain rhythm, one that was dictated by the sun and the sounds of the village. I woke each morning with the first light, my eyes drawn to the soft tendrils of mist that crept through the trees outside my cottage window. As the sun climbed higher, its golden warmth banishing the last remnants of night, I would rise from my bed and prepare myself for the day ahead.

"Another day to fill," I murmured to myself as I went about my morning routine. I had become accustomed to the quiet solitude of my new life, but the weight of it still pressed upon me at times.

I took solace in my daily walks through the woods that surrounded the village, their leafy embrace providing a sanctuary from the curious gazes of my neighbors. The trees whispered secrets to me in the rustling of their leaves, and the birds sang songs that seemed to echo the melancholy that had taken up residence in my heart.

"Will I ever find my place here?" I wondered, my feet following well-worn paths that crisscrossed the forest floor. "Or will I forever be a stranger to myself?"

Returning to my cottage each afternoon, I sought refuge in the pages of books and the melodies of music. My old art supplies gathered dust in a corner, a painful reminder of the life I had left behind. Yet, I could not bring myself to dispose of them – a small part of me clung to the hope that one day, inspiration might strike again.

"Perhaps the muse has forsaken me," I mused, running my fingers over the spines of my books. "Or perhaps she simply bides her time, waiting for the moment when I am ready to listen once more."

As the sun dipped below the horizon, casting the world in hues of amber and crimson, I often found myself standing at the edge of the lake, staring at the ripples that danced upon its surface. The beauty of the scene was not lost on me, and yet it only served to deepen the sense of isolation that gnawed at my soul.

"Is this what I wanted?" I asked myself as tears pricked at the corners of my eyes, the cool breeze carrying them away before they could fall. "To be alone, surrounded by beauty but unable to share it with anyone?"

Night would descend like a velvet shroud, wrapping the village in darkness punctuated only by the flickering glow of lamplight from the windows of the nearby houses. I would retreat to my cottage, sinking into sleep and dreams that were haunted by the ghosts of my past: the brushstrokes on a canvas, the scent of oil paint, the sound of applause ringing in my ears.

"Am I truly lost, or have I simply lost sight of who I am?" I whispered into the darkness, my voice barely audible above the wind's mournful sighs.

But the answer, if there was one, remained elusive – hidden within the shadows that filled my heart.

As I wandered through the village's local market one morning, I was gripped by a sudden longing to experience the creative process once more. The vibrant colors of the fruits and vegetables, the jovial chatter of people around me – it all reminded me of the energy that had once flowed through my veins as I stood before an empty canvas, ready to unleash my talent upon the world.

"Antonia? Antonia Pageta?" A voice called out, jolting me from my reverie. I turned to see a man approaching, his eyes wide with recognition.

"Tom," I said, surprised to see the familiar face. He was a local artist whose work I had admired for its simplicity and sincerity.

"I can't believe it's really you," Tom exclaimed, his cheeks flushing with excitement. "I've been following your work for years. Your paintings are unlike anything I've ever seen before. They're... transcendent."

"Thank you," I murmured, taken aback by his enthusiasm. "But I'm afraid those days are behind me. I've given up on creating art."

"Antonia, no! Why would you do such a thing?" Tom asked, genuine concern etched upon his face.

"Sometimes, the weight of expectations is too much to bear," I explained, my voice trembling with emotion. "The art world can be cruel and unforgiving, and I found myself feeling trapped... suffocated. So, I chose to walk away."

"True," Tom agreed, nodding solemnly. "But you mustn't let that extinguish the fire that burns within you. The world needs your art, Antonia. It's a gift – not just to yourself, but to everyone who experiences it."

I looked into his eyes, searching for any hint of insincerity, but found none. His words stirred something within me – a flicker of hope that had long been dormant.

"Listen," Tom said, taking my hand in his and squeezing it gently. "I have a studio not far from here. It's nothing fancy, just a small space filled with paints and brushes and all the tools you'd need to create your next masterpiece. I want you to use it as much as you like. No expectations, no pressure... just a chance for you to rediscover the joy of creation."

"Are you sure?" I whispered, feeling a surge of gratitude and disbelief.

"Absolutely," he replied with a warm smile. "It would be an honor to help you find your way back to the canvas."

As we walked toward Tom's studio, his kindness and encouragement echoed in my ears, nurturing the fragile ember of hope that had begun to glow within me. For the first time since I had arrived in this quiet village, the prospect of creating art once more didn't seem like an impossible dream.

I hesitated at the entrance to Tom's studio, my heart pounding as memories of my past life in the art world surged through me. The scent of oil paint and turpentine filled my nostrils, both invigorating and terrifying in equal measure. I glanced at Tom, who offered an encouraging smile, and then took a deep breath before stepping over the threshold.

"Welcome to your new sanctuary," he said, gesturing around the space with pride. It was a simple room with large windows that let in ample sunlight, and walls adorned with his own artwork – vibrant landscapes of the village and its surrounding countryside. I couldn't help but feel the pull, the yearning to create once more.

Days turned into weeks, and with each brushstroke, my confidence grew. I began to experiment with new techniques, incorporating the textures and colors I discovered while exploring the village and its lush surroundings. The earthy browns of the soil, the vibrant greens of the rolling hills, and the delicate blues and purples of the wildflowers all found their way onto my canvas.

"Your work is truly breathtaking," Tom remarked one afternoon as he studied my latest piece – a swirling abstract inspired by the rippling surface of the nearby lake. "There's a depth to it that I've never seen before. It's as if you're pouring your soul into every stroke."

"Thank you," I whispered, feeling a flush of warmth spread across my cheeks. His words served as a balm to the wounds left by the art world's betrayal – healing them bit by bit until they became nothing more than faint scars in my memory.

As the months passed, I felt a renewed sense of purpose taking root within me. I no longer painted for recognition or accolades; I painted for myself, and for the sheer joy of capturing the beauty of the world around me. The male hierarchical structure that had once stifled my creativity now felt like a distant nightmare, replaced by the tranquility of my new life in this quiet village.

"Antonia," Tom said one morning as we shared a pot of tea in his small kitchen. "I've been thinking. There's a local art exhibition coming up, and I believe it would be the perfect opportunity for you to showcase your new collection. People need to see what you've been working on."

My heart skipped a beat at the prospect – both thrilling and terrifying. I hesitated, memories of my past experiences in the art world threatening to resurface.

"You don't have to decide now," he reassured me gently, seeming to sense my inner turmoil. "Just think about it."

And so, I did. As I wandered through the village, admiring its quaint charm and natural beauty, I weighed my options. I thought about the person I had become since leaving the art world behind – stronger, more resilient, and fiercely dedicated to my craft. And I realized that my legacy as an artist was far from over; it was only just beginning.

"Tom," I said later that day, my voice filled with determination. "I want to do it – I'll showcase my work at the exhibition."

"Brilliant!" he exclaimed, his eyes shining with pride. "Antonia, I have no doubt that your art will take the world by storm once again."

Only this time, I knew it would be on my own terms – free from the shackles of a world that had once sought to control me. My journey as an artist was not over, but rather, reborn anew amid the idyllic serenity of my newfound sanctuary.

CHAPTER 11

It wasn't long before my inner demons returned. The sun had begun to set, casting long shadows across the dusty cobblestone streets of the small Lake District village I called home. The warm orange glow illuminated every nook and cranny, but somehow managed to evade the dark corners of my heart. It was as if the world was closing in on me, swallowing me whole in its vast emptiness.

Around me, the village seemed to be frozen in time, as though it were a painting rather than a living, breathing place. The houses, with their peeling paint and cracked walls, stood like silent guardians over the empty streets. A stray cat slunk past, its eyes flickering with a mix of curiosity and suspicion as it disappeared into an alleyway. There was a stillness in the air that only amplified my sense of isolation and loneliness.

"Antonia," I whispered to myself, "pull yourself together. You can't let this consume you."

It wasn't just the physical isolation that plagued me; it was the emotional turmoil that accompanied it. As an artist, I yearned for connection, for understanding, for someone to see the world through my eyes - but all I found was solitude. I began to pace back and forth in the cramped room where I spent most of my days, my thoughts racing, my fingers drumming against my thigh.

"Is this all there is?" I muttered, pausing by the window to gaze out at the seemingly endless expanse of rooftops. "Am I destined to spend my life trapped within these four walls, unheard, unseen, unloved?"

I wanted to scream at the injustice of it all - at the fact that my art, the very essence of who I was, remained hidden from the world due to the narrow-mindedness of those around me. I wanted to break free from the chains that bound me, to soar through the skies and let my creativity flow through me, uninhibited.

"Antonia," I chided myself, "you cannot change the world, but you can choose how you face it."

Slowly, I sank to the floor, my back pressed against the cold stone wall. My heart felt heavy in my chest, weighed down by the knowledge that I was alone in my fight. But even as the tendrils of despair threatened to consume me, a spark of determination ignited within my soul, fueled by my unwavering commitment to my artistic vision.

"Maybe I am alone," I whispered, my voice barely audible even to my own ears. "But I will not let them win. I will not let them stifle my creativity, my passion, my spirit. I will find a way to share my art with the world - no matter what it takes."

The depth of my despair plunged deeper than the darkness that enveloped me. My breaths came out strained, each exhale a pang of loneliness echoing through the cold room. The silence was heavy, suffocating; the subtle ticking of the clock on the wall taunted me with its unfaltering progress. I looked at my hands, stained by years of paint and determination, and felt my resolve crack under the weight of sorrow.

"Please," I whispered into the void, my voice cracking as I tried to hold back tears. "I just want to create."

My mind wandered back to a time when my artistic spirit was free, unfettered by the constraints of society and expectations. I remembered the sun-drenched fields, the vibrant colors of poppies and sunflowers stretching towards the azure sky, a symphony of hues that only nature could compose. There I had stood, easel before me, palette in hand, as I translated the beauty before me onto canvas.

"Antonia!" A familiar voice called out in my mind, cutting through the memory like a knife. It was Giovanni, my dearest friend and confidante. "Come, the light is perfect. Let's paint together!"

We spent hours creating side by side, our laughter carried away by the soft summer breeze. In those moments, we were invincible, bound by our passion for art and our unbreakable bond of friendship. The world was ours to explore, one brushstroke at a time.

"Giovanni," I whispered, my heart aching with longing for those simpler times. "I wish you were here."

With a shuddering breath, I rose from the floor, my legs trembling beneath me. I wiped the tears from my cheeks, leaving streaks of pain behind. I knew I had no choice but to forge ahead, to keep my artistic spirit alive despite the crushing burden of isolation and despair.

"Art is my life," I murmured, clenching my fists. "No matter the cost, I will find a way to create and share my vision with the world."

Resolve settled like armor around me, hardening my determination. My artistic spirit would not be defeated, no matter how desolate my surroundings or how deep my loneliness. For in the end, it was my passion for creation that would carry me through even the darkest of nights.

Night had fallen, and the house lay silent around me. I crept down the dim hallway to the small room at the back of the house – my secret sanctuary. A feeling of freedom washed over me as I closed the door behind me and locked it with a soft click.

"Finally," I sighed, allowing myself a moment to revel in the solitude. "It's just you and me now."

Surrounded by my art supplies – a hodgepodge collection of salvaged paintbrushes, jars of pigments, and makeshift canvases – I felt a renewed sense of purpose. Despite the darkness that threatened to consume me, I would not let it extinguish my artistic fire.

"Time to bring you to life," I whispered, my fingers tracing the outline of the figure on the canvas before me. My heart raced as I picked up a brush, dipped it into the vibrant blue pigment, and began to paint.

As the hours slipped away, I lost myself in the process of creation. The scratchy strokes of my brush against the canvas, the intoxicating scent of oil paints, the weight of emotions pouring from my hand – all of it served as my lifeline amid the crushing isolation.

"Antonia," I scolded myself, pausing for a moment to catch my breath. "You are stronger than this loneliness. You must keep going."

I continued painting, each stroke more confident than the last. My character took shape on the canvas, her eyes filled with a determination that mirrored my own. She was not only a product of my imagination but also a symbol of my resilience – a testament to my unwavering commitment to my artistic vision.

"Look at you," I said softly, admiring the progress I'd made. "We're creating something beautiful together, despite everything."

In this hidden space, where no one could see or judge my work, I allowed myself to be vulnerable. Each brushstroke was a testament to the love, pain, and loneliness that consumed me. My art became my solace, and in those stolen moments of creation, I found the strength to carry on.

"Even in darkness," I whispered, gazing at my latest masterpiece with pride, "there is light."

The world I painted was one of vibrant colors, surreal landscapes, and dreamlike atmospheres. Each stroke of my brush transported me to this realm, where the sun danced in a sky swirling with hues unseen by human eyes, and the trees whispered their secrets in a language only I could understand.

"Ah, my dear friend," I murmured, running my fingers across the canvas, feeling the texture of painted leaves. "You offer me solace in a time of great despair."

The contrast between the lifeless walls of my isolation and the fantastical creations on my canvas grew starker with each passing day. In my art, there were no boundaries, no limitations – only endless possibilities. It was a place where I was free – free from judgement, free from expectations, and free from the crushing weight of loneliness.

"Antonia," I whispered to myself, dipping my brush into a pool of deep crimson paint. "This is your sanctuary, your haven. Here, you are never truly alone."

As I continued painting, I poured all the dreams and desires that had been locked away into my art. The vibrant colors represented the love I yearned for, the surreal landscapes symbolized my boundless creativity, and the dreamlike atmosphere mirrored the innermost depths of my soul.

"Here, in this world of my own creation," I thought, "I can escape the suffocating confines of my reality. This is where I belong."

With each new piece, I explored the farthest reaches of my imagination, discovering new worlds, new creatures, and new stories. As I filled my hidden sanctuary with these wondrous creations, I felt a sense of pride swell within me.

"Look at what you've accomplished, Antonia," I said to myself, stepping back to admire my latest masterpiece. "Even in the darkest times, you have found a way to create beauty."

The stark contrast between the world I painted and the one in which I lived served as a constant reminder of the importance of my art. It was not just an escape, but a lifeline – a means of survival in a world that seemed determined to break me.

"Through my art," I vowed, gripping my paintbrush tightly, "I will persevere. No matter what challenges lie ahead, I will continue to create – for this is who I am, and this is where I find solace."

In the secret sanctuary of my imagination, surrounded by the fantastical creations that sprung from my brush, I found hope. And with that hope, I carried on, ever-determined to bring the beauty of my inner world to life on canvas.

The sun dipped below the horizon, casting shadows across my small studio. I squeezed a dollop of vibrant red paint onto my palette and began to work feverishly, losing myself in the brushstrokes and colors that flowed from my hand. The final piece of my latest creation was falling into place, and I could feel the anticipation building within me, like a caged bird desperate for release.

"Antonia!" a voice called out from beyond my door, shattering my concentration. Panic surged through me as I realized the precarious position I now found myself in. My secret, my art, was at risk of being discovered.

"Uh, one moment!" I stammered, grabbing a dusty cloth from the table and hurriedly draping it over my latest masterpiece. My heart pounded in my chest as I fumbled with the lock on the old wooden door, the knob slick with sweat under my fingertips.

"Is everything alright in there?" the voice asked, concern lacing the words. It was Tom, my kind-hearted neighbor who often checked up on me. He had no idea of the world I had created within these walls, or the lengths I went to protect it. He wouldn't understand that I couldn't share this with anyone, not yet.

"Y-yes, just give me a second," I replied, hastily wiping paint from my hands onto my apron. I took a deep breath, attempting to compose myself before opening the door. When I finally did, the scent of fresh bread and warm spices wafted in from Tom's kitchen.

"Antonia, dear, I thought you might be hungry, so I brought you some dinner," he said, offering me a steaming bowl of pasta. His eyes flickered to the cloth-covered canvas behind me, curiosity and suspicion mingling in his gaze. "I didn't mean to interrupt your...whatever it is you're doing."

"Thank you, Tom," I said, forcing a weak smile. "I was just...cleaning up a bit." I took the bowl from him and quickly closed the door behind me, my heart still racing in my throat.

As I sat down to eat the meal Tom had so kindly provided, my thoughts were consumed by the close call. It was becoming increasingly difficult to keep my secret hidden, even from those who cared for me. The weight of this burden pressed heavily on my chest, threatening to consume me entirely.

Later that night, after locking the door once more and ensuring my art remained safely concealed, I returned to my easel. As I lifted my paintbrush, the tension in my body dissipated, replaced by a sense of freedom and exhilaration. With each stroke of vibrant color, my fears and anxieties seemed to melt away, leaving only the pure joy of creation.

"Let it out, Antonia," I whispered to myself as I allowed my imagination to take control, guiding my hand across the canvas. "This is where you find your peace."

As the final brushstroke fell into place, a feeling of immense satisfaction washed over me. I stepped back, taking in the entirety of my creation. It was a world unlike any other – a dreamscape filled with whimsical creatures and lush, otherworldly landscapes. A world that belonged solely to me.

In that moment, standing before the product of my passion and determination, I knew that no matter the cost, I could never abandon my art. It was my lifeline, my escape from the crushing weight of reality. And despite the risks, I vowed to continue creating, for in my art, I found solace – and in that solace, I found hope.

Days turned to weeks, and my small attic studio became a sanctuary where I could lose myself in the intricate details of my art. Yet, as I painted, the shadows of doubt crept into every corner, threatening my newfound peace. Would someone discover my secret? Was it worth the risk?

"Antonia," I whispered aloud, as if speaking to myself might bring some clarity to the storm brewing inside me. "You were born for this. You cannot let fear rule you."

One day, as I stood at my easel, lost in the surreal landscape before me, a sudden knock on the door startled me back to reality. My heart pounded in my chest, and I instinctively reached for the cloth to cover my work.

"Antonia, are you in there?" Again it was Tom, his voice muffled by the wooden barrier between us.

"Si, Tom." My voice trembled with trepidation. "Just a moment, please."

With swift, calculated movements, I hid my latest piece beneath a pile of discarded canvases. The incessant knocking continued, growing more impatient with each passing second. As I unlocked the door and swung it open, I braced myself for the onslaught of questions that would inevitably follow.

"Antonia, what's going on? Why is this door always locked now?" His eyes darted around the room, searching for answers I was not ready to give.

"Nothing, Tom. I just need some privacy sometimes," I replied, attempting to feign nonchalance. My hands clenched at my sides, desperate to maintain control over the situation.

"Privacy? For what?" He raised an eyebrow, skepticism etched across his face.

"Tom, please," I pleaded, my eyes fixating on his, willing him to understand. "I have my reasons."

For a moment, we stood in silence, staring at one another. Then, with a sigh, Tom nodded. "Alright, Antonia. I won't pry. But if you need to talk, I'm here for you."

"Thank you." Relief washed over me as I pulled him into a tight embrace.

As he left, my resolve hardened. I knew that continuing my art in secrecy would be a battle, but it was a battle I was willing to fight.

Returning to my easel, I picked up my paintbrush and let the rich colors flow onto the canvas. Each stroke was a testament to my determination, a declaration that I would not be held down by fear or uncertainty.

And as the sun dipped below the horizon, casting its warm, golden light through the small attic window, I felt a renewed sense of hope. For now, my secret remained safe – and so did my dreams.

CHAPTER 12

The weight of the world seemed to rest on my shoulders as I dipped my paintbrush into a pool of vibrant red paint. My name is Antonia Pageta, and I am an artist - a struggling one at that. I could feel the stress gnawing away at my health, bit by agonizing bit. Some days, it was all too much; but then again, this life was never meant to be easy.

"Antonia, darling, are you sure you're okay?" my best friend, Tom, asked with a concerned look on his face. "You look paler than usual."

"Ah, don't worry about me," I replied, forcing a smile. As I turned my attention back to the canvas in front of me, I couldn't help but remember the hurdles I had faced throughout my journey as an artist. Each brushstroke felt like a battle scar earned from a lifetime of struggles.

I recalled the countless nights I spent hunched over my work, trying to make ends meet with every painting sold. The long hours were taking their toll on my body, and the financial strain was only adding to my mounting stress. It felt as if I was caught in a vicious cycle: An endless loop of sleepless nights, unpaid bills, and creative blocks.

Then there were the relationships that crumbled under the weight of my ambitions. Lovers who couldn't understand my need for solitude and dedication to my art, leaving me feeling even more isolated than before. And yet, despite everything, I refused to let go of my dreams. Surrealism was my passion, my guiding light through the darkest of times.

"Antonia, are you listening?" Tom's voice snapped me out of my reverie. "I'm worried about you. Your health is declining, and I can see it's affecting your art, too."

"Thank you, Tom, but I'll be fine," I insisted, dipping my brush into a soothing shade of blue. "I won't let this beat me. I'll keep going, no matter what."

The pain struck again, like a hammer pounding on my temple. I winced, gripping my paintbrush tighter as the migraine intensified. It had become an unwelcome companion, accompanying me throughout my days and nights. The migraines were often followed by panic attacks that left me gasping for air, my heart racing as if it was trying to escape my chest.

"Antonia, have you taken your medication?" Tom's concerned voice brought me back to reality. "You look pale."

I shook my head, still clutching the paintbrush. "I can't, it makes me too drowsy," I muttered, focusing on the canvas in front of me. "I need to finish this piece."

"Your health is more important than finishing a painting," he retorted. "You've been pushing yourself too hard lately."

I sighed, knowing he was right. But what choice did I have? My art was my life, and if I couldn't produce it, everything would fall apart. "Tom, I appreciate your concern, but I'll be okay," I said, trying to sound more convincing than I felt.

As I tried to immerse myself in my work, my thoughts drifted towards the plans I'd canceled with family and friends. Birthdays, gatherings, holidays – all missed because of my declining health. I could see the hurt in their eyes when I made yet another excuse, and their patience wearing thin. Deep down, I feared they would give up on me eventually, leaving me truly alone.

"Antonia," Tom began hesitantly, "maybe you should consider taking a break. You know, spend some time with your loved ones, or just rest."

"Can't afford to," I whispered, the weight of my situation pressing down on me. "I need to keep going."

"Is it worth sacrificing everything?" he asked, sadness evident in his voice.

I paused, the paintbrush hovering over the canvas. Was it worth it? The constant pain, the strained relationships, the overwhelming exhaustion? In that moment, I realized how much my health struggles had consumed me, and the sacrifices I'd made for my art. But fear of failure kept me tethered to this path, unsure of any other way forward.

"Maybe it's not," I admitted softly, finally allowing myself to acknowledge the truth. "But right now, I don't know what else to do."

The sun dipped below the horizon, casting an eerie glow on my half-finished canvas. I had been working for hours, ignoring the throbbing pain in my temples and the fatigue that threatened to swallow me whole. My hands shook as I clutched the paintbrush, but my vision was clear – a surreal dreamscape that poured from my soul onto the canvas.

"Antonia," a familiar voice called out softly from behind me, "it's getting late. Maybe you should rest."

"Can't," I muttered, willing myself to focus on the canvas before me. The colors swirled together, creating a world that only I could see. "Not until this is finished."

"Your health is more important than your art," Tom said gently, his concern palpable. He knew how much I struggled with chronic fatigue and migraines, but he also understood my unwavering dedication to my craft.

"Art is what keeps me going, Tom," I replied, my voice strained with exhaustion. "If I stop now, I feel like I'll lose everything."

"Have you considered that maybe it's not just about the art?" he asked, his eyes searching mine for understanding. "Maybe there's something deeper that needs healing."

I sighed, feeling the weight of his words. I knew he was right, but admitting it would mean facing the reality of my situation — a reality I wasn't ready to confront. "I won't let this beat me," I whispered, determination flooding through me. "I'll keep going no matter what."

"Promise me you'll take care of yourself, Antonia," Tom implored, his eyes brimming with tears. "You don't have to face this alone."

My heart clenched at her words, knowing that my health struggles were not only my burden to bear, but also those who cared for me. "I promise," I said softly, the words feeling like a fragile truce.

As Tom left me to my work, I stared at the canvas before me, the surreal landscape a reflection of my inner turmoil. The vibrant colors mixed with dark shadows, a testament to both my passion and my pain. With each brushstroke, I felt the weight of my struggles lessen, if only for a moment.

In that instant, I understood that my art was not only an escape from my reality but also a lifeline that kept me from succumbing to my ailments. And so, I continued to paint, my commitment unwavering, my resilience unbreakable, and my spirit indomitable.

As I dipped my paintbrush into the vibrant hues on my palette, a sudden memory washed over me like a tidal wave. It was a few months ago when I had collapsed from exhaustion in my studio, my body paying the price for weeks of sleepless nights and relentless work.

"Antonia!" I heard Tom's voice echo through my mind, his panic palpable as he rushed to my side. "You need to rest."

I could still feel the cold concrete beneath me, the weakness in my limbs, and the taste of iron in my mouth. The sensation of helplessness threatened to pull me under, but I fought against it, focusing on the canvas before me.

"Deep breaths, Antonia," I muttered to myself, remembering the advice Tom had given me during one of my panic attacks. My chest tightened, the familiar feeling of anxiety creeping in like an unwanted visitor. I closed my eyes, taking slow, deliberate breaths, trying to calm my racing heart. I could hear the blood pulsing in my ears, drowning out all other sounds.

"Focus on your art, Antonia," I whispered, willing myself to regain control of my emotions. "Let it guide you through this storm."

As I opened my eyes and looked at the canvas, I noticed my hand trembling ever so slightly. I clenched my fist, steadying myself before continuing with my brushstrokes. With each stroke, my breathing began to normalize, and my heart rate slowed.

"See?" I told myself, a small smile tugging at the corners of my lips. "You can do this."

As I continued to paint, I felt the weight of my past struggles slowly dissipate, replaced by a sense of purpose and determination. I refused to let my health dictate my life or hinder my passion.

Weeks later, I found myself sitting in my small studio, surrounded by half-finished paintings and crumpled sketches. The scent of oil paint and turpentine hung heavy in the air, a comforting reminder of countless hours spent here, immersed in my work. But today, it did little to ease the gnawing frustration that tightened around my chest like a vice.

"Damn it!" I cursed under my breath as I stared at the canvas before me. My once sure and steady hand now shook with each brushstroke, making it nearly impossible to capture the finer details of my vision. The colors on the palette seemed dull and lifeless, mocking my futile attempts to breathe life into them. A sense of futility washed over me like an icy wave, leaving me shivering and defeated.

"Antonia, are you alright?" Tom's concerned voice broke through my thoughts as he entered the room. His eyes widened at the sight of me slumped over in my chair, my head cradled in my hands.

"Look at this," I muttered bitterly, gesturing to the chaotic mess on the canvas. "I can't even hold a brush steady anymore. What kind of artist am I if I can't create?"

Tom hesitated before tentatively placing a hand on my shoulder. "You're still an incredible artist, Antonia. This is just a rough patch. We all have them."

"Rough patch?" I scoffed, tears welling up in my eyes. "This is more than just a rough patch, Tom. My health is spiraling out of control, and it's taking my art with it. I'm so tired...so tired of fighting."

"Hey, hey," Tom whispered, pulling me into a tight embrace. "I know it's hard, but you can't give up. Your art means too much to you, to all of us. You're stronger than this, Antonia, I know you are."

As I clung to Tom, sobbing into his shoulder, I couldn't help but feel a small flame of hope flicker within me. I had always been a fighter, and while my body may betray me at times, my spirit remained unbroken.

"Thank you, Tom," I murmured, wiping away the tears that stained my cheeks. "You're right. I won't let this defeat me. I'll find a way to create, even if it's not the same as before."

With newfound determination, I picked up my brush once more, refusing to allow my health to dictate my passion. I would adapt, overcome, and continue to push the boundaries of my art, no matter the obstacles in my path.

I stood before my easel, my heart heavy and throbbing like an anvil in my chest. It was as if the weight of my health struggles had manifested into a physical burden, pressing down on my shoulders and threatening to crush me beneath its oppressive force. The canvas stared back at me, its pristine whiteness taunting my inability to bring my vision to life.

"Antonia!" a familiar voice called out, startling me from my thoughts. It was a vision of my friend, Giovanni, as he entered my studio, his brow furrowed with concern. "Are you alright?"

"Giovanni," I sighed, placing my brush down onto the palette. "Sometimes it feels like I'm drowning in my own body. My pain and fatigue are like the water, filling my lungs and suffocating my creativity."

"Antonia, you can't let this define you," he implored, resting a hand on my shoulder. "You're so much more than your illness."

"Am I?" I questioned, feeling the sting of doubt prickling at my resolve. "What good is an artist who cannot create?"

"An artist who doesn't give up," Giovanni replied, his eyes full of determination. "You've never been one to back down from a challenge, Antonia. Don't start now."

Despite my frustration, I couldn't help but smile at his unwavering belief in me. His words sparked something within me, a fire that refused to be extinguished by the cold tide of pain and fatigue.

"Okay," I whispered, taking a deep breath and picking up my brush once more. "I'll keep fighting, Giovanni. I won't give up."

"Good," he encouraged, stepping back to give me space, my vision of him fading, growing softer. "Now show me what you're made of, Antonia Pageta. Make this canvas sing."

And so, I did. Ignoring the relentless ache in my body, I let the fire within me guide my brush, each stroke a testament to my resilience. The weight on my shoulders began to lift, if only slightly, as I allowed myself to become lost in the world of color and form.

My art was my lifeline, my salvation. And though my health might waver, my spirit would remain unbroken, for I was Antonia Pageta – the artist who refused to be defeated by her own body.

CHAPTER 13

Surrounded by the vibrant colors and surreal shapes of my paintings, I sat on the worn wooden stool in the center of my studio. The smell of oil paint and turpentine hung heavy in the air, and the sound of my own breathing echoed softly off the high ceilings. But it was not the familiar surroundings that consumed my thoughts; it was the incredible journey that had led me to this very moment.

As I gazed around at my artwork, each piece told a story - not only of the subject matter but also of my life as an artist. My brow furrowed as I remembered the countless hours spent perfecting every brushstroke, every line, every shadow. And with that memory came a flood of emotions: the frustration, the heartache, the moments when I felt like giving up. But somehow, I didn't. Tears welled up in my eyes, a mix of pain and triumph, sadness and joy.

"Antonia," I whispered to myself, "how did you manage to survive all these years through so much turmoil?" It was a question that weighed heavily on my mind. In the quiet sanctuary of my studio, I allowed myself to delve into memories long buried beneath the veneer of success. I recalled the tiny village in Italy where I was born, where my passion for art first began to take root. I remembered the setbacks and challenges I faced along the way, the people who doubted me, and those precious few who believed in me.

"Look at you now, Antonia," I murmured between sobs. "You've come so far." Despite the tears streaming down my cheeks, a small, proud smile began to form on my lips. For amidst the trials and tribulations that had shaped my life, there were shining moments of accomplishment that could not be denied - the first time a stranger purchased one of my paintings, the overwhelming joy of winning my first award, the awe and wonder in the eyes of those who viewed my work.

"Your journey has been a remarkable one," I told myself, wiping away the tears from my cheeks. "And it's far from over." With a deep breath, I rose from my stool, my heart swelling with gratitude for all that I had overcome and accomplished. As the sun began to set, casting a warm glow over my studio, I felt my spirit soar, renewed and ready to continue creating. For I knew that no matter what challenges lay ahead, my art would always be my guiding light, and my legacy would endure through the ages.

As I sat amidst the array of colorful canvases, scattered paintbrushes and sculptures, my thoughts drifted toward the tremendous growth I had experienced throughout my life. I recalled the timid girl who would secretly sketch in her bedroom after midnight, fearful of her family's disapproval. The same girl who, with time, had blossomed into a daring woman unafraid to pursue her dreams. How far I had come.

"Antonia," I whispered to myself, "you've truly evolved." My fingers traced the rough edges of the canvas before me, a testament to the countless hours spent perfecting my craft. Every stroke, every shade, every layer represented years of dedication and experimentation. It was through these trials that my artistic voice had emerged, strong and clear.

"Look at what you've accomplished," I mused, reminiscing about the prestigious awards that adorned the walls of my studio. Each one held a story, a precious memory of triumph that fueled my passion. I could still hear the applause echoing in my ears as I accepted each accolade, the shimmering golden statues clutched tightly in my hands. These were more than mere trophies; they were symbols of my impact on the art world.

"Your work has graced the walls of renowned galleries," I reminded myself, the memories flooding back like a tidal wave. From the bustling metropolis of New York City to the romantic streets of Paris, my creations had been displayed for all to see. I remembered the thrill of seeing my name etched on a small plaque beside my artwork, the pride swelling within me as strangers marveled at my creations.

"Who would have thought that little Antonia from Italy would make such waves?" I chuckled softly, shaking my head in disbelief. Yet there it was, undeniable proof of my influence and my place in the annals of art history.

"Keep pushing forward, Antonia," I urged myself, determination surging through my veins. "Your journey is far from over." As I picked up my paintbrush and dipped it into a vibrant hue, I knew that no matter what lay ahead, my passion for my art would carry me through. And with each new masterpiece, my legacy would continue to grow and inspire generations to come.

"Antonia, your work has been an inspiration to me," I recalled a young artist telling me at one of my exhibitions. She had gazed at my paintings with wide-eyed admiration, her enthusiasm contagious. "You've shown me that it's possible to break boundaries and defy expectations."

"Thank you," I responded, genuinely touched by her words. It was in moments like these that I realized the true power of art – the ability to connect with others on a deeply personal level, to evoke emotions, and to inspire change.

My mind wandered to other instances where my work had sparked important conversations about social issues. One particular piece came to mind: a surrealist portrait of a woman, half of her face hidden behind a veil, struggling to break free from societal constraints. Critics praised it for challenging traditional gender roles and igniting discussions about women's rights.

"Your art speaks to the heart of our shared human experience," said one critic during a panel discussion. His words resonated within me, filling me with a deep sense of pride and gratitude for the impact my creations had on the world.

"Is this really happening?" I whispered to myself, tears welling up in my eyes. I was overcome with a sense of fulfillment; my work had transcended the confines of my studio and reached out to touch the lives of countless individuals.

"Your legacy will be remembered, Antonia," I told myself, wiping away a stray tear. "Not just for the beauty of your artwork, but for the powerful messages they conveyed."

"Thank you," I murmured, words of gratitude directed not only to those who had supported me along the way, but to the universe itself – for granting me the gift of creativity and the opportunity to make a difference.

"Your work has changed the way I see the world," another admirer once confessed, their voice trembling with emotion. "You've taught me to question the status quo and to seek out beauty in the most unexpected places."

"Keep creating, Antonia," I urged myself, my heart swelling with pride as I thought of all those who had found solace, inspiration, or empowerment through my art. "Your work has the power to change lives – never forget that."

And so, I continued on my artistic journey, fueled by a renewed sense of purpose and passion. As I picked up my paintbrush, the vibrant colors swirling onto the canvas before me, I knew that each new piece would carry the weight of my legacy – and, in turn, inspire countless others to follow their own dreams.

"Thank you for everything, Antonia Pageta," I whispered, a smile tugging at the corners of my lips. "Your impact on the art world is immeasurable, and your influence will be felt for generations to come."

As I sat in the comforting silence of my studio, surrounded by the tangible manifestations of my life's work, I allowed myself to envision what the future might hold. The thought of future generations walking through hallowed halls, admiring my artwork and learning from my experiences brought me a profound sense of solace.

"Imagine them, Antonia," I whispered to myself, visualizing art enthusiasts gazing at my paintings with awe and curiosity, their faces illuminated by the soft glow of gallery lights. "They will study your technique, marvel at your vision, and dissect the meaning behind each brushstroke."

The notion that my work would not be forgotten – that it would continue to live on long after I had taken my last breath – filled me with a contentment I could hardly put into words. It was as if all the struggles, sacrifices, and moments of doubt had been worth it; for this, if nothing else, was my gift to the world.

"Your art will be preserved, Antonia," I murmured, allowing myself to bask in the warmth of that thought. "Museums and galleries will keep your creations safe for years to come, ensuring that they remain a testament to your talent and dedication."

"Thank you," I said aloud, feeling tears prick at the corners of my eyes. "Thank you for allowing me to leave something behind – a legacy that speaks not only to who I am but also to the power of art itself."

I took a deep breath, my chest swelling with a mixture of pride and gratitude. As I exhaled, I felt an overwhelming sense of peace wash over me, like a wave gently lapping at the shore.

"Antonia Pageta," I whispered, my voice barely audible above the quiet rustle of paintbrushes and canvas. "You have truly made your mark on this world, and your legacy will continue to inspire others for generations to come."

I smiled, my heart filled with a sense of fulfillment that I would carry with me every day from then on. With renewed vigor, I picked up my paintbrush and turned my attention back to the canvas before me, ready to create something new – something that would become a part of my enduring legacy.

"Here's to the future," I murmured, feeling the weight of history in each stroke of my brush. "May it be as vibrant, bold, and beautiful as the art I leave behind."

With a sense of peace now enveloping me, I took a deep breath and allowed a gentle smile to grace my lips. My thoughts wandered through the myriad of memories that made up the tapestry of my life – each one precious, significant, and a testament to my journey.

I recalled the first time I sold a painting. It was a small piece depicting a vibrant sunset over the humble village where I was born. The gallery owner had been kind but firm in his critique of my work, offering a modest sum for it. I remember feeling a mixture of pride and disbelief as I handed over the painting, realizing that someone had seen value in my art.

"The world will know your name, Antonia," he had said, his words resonating with me long after our exchange.

My heart swelled at the memory, and then shifted to another pivotal moment in my career – the creation of "La Speranza" or "Hope" – a piece that challenged me in ways I could never have anticipated. It was during a particularly tumultuous time in my life when I had lost someone dear to me, and I found solace in translating my pain into a visual representation.

"Hope" became a deeply personal and cathartic experience, pushing me to explore new techniques and uncharted emotional depths. The countless hours spent refining every detail, the frustration of starting anew when things didn't feel right, and ultimately, the triumph of capturing the essence of hope amidst despair — all these experiences taught me the importance of perseverance and staying true to my artistic vision.

"Antonia, you are capable of greatness," I whispered to myself, remembering the overwhelming sense of accomplishment I felt when that piece was finally unveiled to the world.

These memories and more filled me with gratitude and a newfound appreciation for the path I had chosen. I knew that my life's work would continue to resonate with others, even after I was gone, and that thought brought me immense comfort. It was as if my art had become a living, breathing entity — a part of me that would endure beyond the confines of time.

"Your legacy will live on, Antonia Pageta," I murmured softly, the weight of those words settling deep within my heart.

As I stood in the comforting embrace of my studio, surrounded by the fruits of my labor, I knew that I had found my purpose, my passion, and ultimately, my peace. And with that knowledge, I could continue to create, knowing that each brushstroke, each line, and each hue would tell a story — my story — for generations to come.

My mind wandered, my gaze shifting from one canvas to another. Each work of art was a symphony of colors and textures, a testament to the years I had spent honing my craft. The smell of oil paint and turpentine filled the air, mingling with the soft hum of the overhead lights. The sound of my own breathing echoed in the otherwise silent studio — a space that had borne witness to countless moments of inspiration, frustration, and triumph.

"Ah, La Danza della Morte," I murmured, my eyes resting on a painting I had created many years ago. The vibrant hues of red and orange seemed to dance across the canvas, depicting the eternal struggle between life and death. I recalled how the smooth surface of the canvas had given way beneath the pressure of my brush, each stroke leaving behind a trail of color that would soon form a world of its own.

"Quanto tempo è passato?" I whispered, as I traced my fingers over the rough texture of another piece — a portrait of a young woman, her face etched with an expression of quiet defiance. I remembered the hours I had spent laboring over every detail, my hand guided by the intricate dance of light and shadow that played upon her features. The memory of her laughter, like the sweetest melody, still lingered in my ears.

"Ma quanto sei cresciuta, Antonia," I said softly, my voice barely audible above the gentle rustle of my paintbrush against the canvas. The words were a testament to the growth I had experienced throughout my life — not just as an artist, but as a person.

I felt a tear escape my eye, the warm droplet slipping down my cheek and splashing onto the polished wooden floor. As I wiped it away, I could not help but marvel at the journey that had led me to this moment — the challenges I had faced, the barriers I had broken, and the dreams I had dared to chase.

"Non finisce qui," I vowed, my voice filled with conviction. My story was far from over, and neither was my art. With a deep breath, I straightened my back and stretched my arms above my head, feeling the tension in my muscles dissipate. A renewed sense of purpose coursed through me, urging me to continue creating.

"Avanti, Antonia," I whispered, a smile tugging at the corners of my lips. "La tua storia deve continuare."

And so, with brush in hand and heart full of determination, I returned to the easel, ready to immortalize yet another chapter of my life on canvas — for the world to see, to remember, and to cherish.

CHAPTER 14

"An unexpected turn" could be the title of my life. I, Anthony Padgett, an artist from England, thought I knew where I was going, but life has a funny way of changing one's direction.

The abandoned warehouse district in Lancashire wasn't exactly where I had planned to spend my Saturday afternoon. Rather, I'd intended to visit the studios of local artists for inspiration. But here I was, stepping over broken glass and tattered debris, unable to resist the allure of exploring these forgotten structures.

"Anthony, you're crazy," I muttered to myself as I carefully navigated the darkened rooms of an old warehouse. The smell of aged wood and rust filled my nostrils, bringing with it a sense of history and decay. I felt like I was trespassing on someone else's life, but curiosity propelled me forward.

"Whoa." My heart caught in my throat when I stumbled upon a hidden room within the building. A dusty, cracked window let in just enough light to illuminate the space, revealing an old, makeshift studio.

"Antonia Pageta" was written in faded black ink on a half-torn label attached to a worn leather portfolio. I opened it gently, uncovering detailed sketches and studies, each more beautiful than the last. In that moment, I felt as if I had discovered a buried treasure. Antonia Pageta, a name I had never heard before, yet her work spoke to me on a level I couldn't quite explain.

"Hey! What are you doing in here?" A gruff voice startled me, and I quickly hid the portfolio behind my back.

"Uh, I was just... exploring," I stammered, feeling a blush creep up my cheeks. "I didn't mean any harm."

"Exploring, huh?" The man, likely the building's caretaker, narrowed his eyes at me suspiciously. "Well, you'd better not be causing any trouble."

"Of course not," I replied earnestly. "I'm an art student, and I just happened upon this studio. It's... incredible."

He raised an eyebrow at my enthusiasm but seemed to relax a bit. "Alright, just be careful. This place is old and falling apart."

"Thank you, sir," I said gratefully, watching as he turned to leave. When he was out of sight, I let out a small sigh of relief and allowed myself to become fully immersed in the world of Antonia Pageta.

As I studied each piece more intensely, I felt a deep connection forming between us, two artists separated by time and circumstance. Antonia's work displayed a kind of raw beauty that stirred something within me. I couldn't walk away now. I needed to learn everything about her and share this discovery with the world.

"Antonia," I whispered to myself, "I won't let your legacy be forgotten."

The dim light from the cracked window in the corner of the studio was barely enough to illuminate the space before me. Dust danced through the air, swirling and settling on every surface like a heavy blanket. I coughed and waved my hand to clear a path for myself, my heart pounding with excitement.

"Wow," I whispered, taking in the cobwebs that draped over everything like delicate lace. The floor was littered with paintings and sculptures, some leaning against the walls, others lying haphazardly on the ground. It was as if someone had left in a hurry, abandoning these masterpieces without a second thought.

I carefully stepped over a cracked sculpture of a woman's torso, marveling at the lifelike detail despite its damaged state. My fingers itched to touch each piece, but I resisted, not wanting to disturb their fragile existence any further.

"Who could have created all this?" I wondered aloud, my voice barely audible even to myself.

"Antonia Pageta," a voice answered from behind me.

"Who?" I spun around, startled by the sudden intrusion.

"Antonia," repeated the caretaker, his gruff exterior softened by an unmistakable reverence for the artist. "She was a surrealist painter, born in Italy. A true genius."

"Her work is incredible," I breathed, my eyes scanning the room again, seeing each piece with newfound appreciation.

"Take a look at this one." The caretaker gestured toward a large canvas resting against the wall, partially obscured by a dusty tarp. I hesitated for a moment before carefully lifting the tarp, revealing the stunning image beneath.

My breath caught in my throat as I gazed upon the face of a woman, her expression a haunting blend of sorrow and strength. Her eyes seemed to pierce through the canvas, reaching deep into my soul.

"Amazing," I whispered, feeling a swell of emotion well up inside me.

"Antonia had a gift for capturing the very essence of her subjects," the caretaker said quietly, his eyes fixed on the painting. "It's a shame the world never got to see her work."

"Wait, what do you mean?" I asked, my curiosity piqued.

"Antonia died young, only 35, from cancer. Her art was rarely exhibited, and she faded into obscurity."

"That's not fair!" I exclaimed, my heart aching for the artist who had poured her soul into these stunning creations. "She deserves to be remembered!"

The caretaker nodded solemnly. "I agree, but the art world can be cruel, and sometimes even the most talented are forgotten."

"Then it's up to us to make sure they're not," I declared, my determination ignited by Antonia's powerful artwork. "I'll do whatever it takes to bring her work into the spotlight."

"Good luck," the caretaker replied, his expression softening with a hint of a smile. "I hope you succeed."

The sun had dipped below the horizon, casting long shadows across Antonia's forgotten studio. As I wandered deeper into the space, time seemed to slow down, allowing me to drink in every detail of her art. It was as if each piece whispered its own story, beckoning me to listen.

"Antonia Pageta," I murmured, running my fingers over a dusty journal cover. Flipping through the fragile pages, I began to piece together the life of this brilliant and resilient artist. Her words painted a picture of a woman who fought against the expectations of society, determined to stay true to her artistic vision.

"Born in a small village in Italy," I read aloud, tracing the lines of a handwritten letter with my fingertips. "A fiercely independent spirit, unyielding in the face of adversity." From her writings, I could sense Antonia's passion for her work, her courage, and her strength. The more I learned about her, the more I felt a connection to this extraordinary woman who had been lost to history.

"Rosa, you've been in here for hours," said the caretaker, his voice breaking through my reverie. "You might want to take a break."

Shaking my head, I replied, "I can't. I need to understand her, to find a way to share Antonia's art with the world."

"Alright. But remember, you still have your own studies to attend to," he cautioned, before leaving me alone once more.

As the night wore on, I continued to immerse myself in Antonia's world, searching for a way to honor her legacy. My heart ached at the thought of her incredible talent being confined to this dimly lit studio, hidden from the eyes of those who would appreciate it the most.

"Antonia, what am I supposed to do?" I whispered, feeling overwhelmed by the task that lay ahead of me. "How can I make sure you are not forgotten?"

In that moment, it felt as if her spirit was with me, urging me to persevere. I knew that I had been entrusted with a great responsibility, and I was determined to see it through.

"Alright," I said, feeling a renewed sense of purpose. "Let's start by finding out everything we can about your life and work."

Over the following weeks, I delved into Antonia's past, painstakingly researching her artistic journey, her influences, and the impact she had on those around her. But in order to truly share her art with others, I realized that I would need to face challenges I never imagined – from restoring her damaged paintings and sculptures to convincing galleries and museums of her worth.

"Antonia, I promise I won't let you down," I vowed, my heart swelling with determination. "Your art deserves to be seen, and your story deserves to be heard."

And so, armed with passion and resolve, I set out on a mission to bring Antonia Pageta's art back into the spotlight – even if it meant risking my own reputation and future as an artist.

The sun dipped below the horizon, casting long shadows across my cluttered apartment. I sat hunched over my laptop, a steaming mug of coffee on one side and a stack of Antonia's journals on the other. The more I learned about her life, the more I became determined to share her story with the world.

"Antonia," I murmured under my breath, "your work deserves the spotlight it never had."

I spent days crafting the perfect email, detailing Antonia's talent and passion for art, along with images of her most striking pieces. Addressing it to a prestigious gallery in London, I hesitated for a moment before pressing 'send.' There was no turning back now.

"Here goes nothing," I whispered, feeling both excitement and dread.

Days later, I received my first reply. My heart raced as I opened the message, only to find that the curator had dismissed Antonia's work as "interesting, but lacking the depth and innovation" they sought for their collection. I clenched my fists, frustration bubbling within me. How could they not see the beauty and raw emotion in Antonia's art?

"Alright," I muttered to myself, "we'll try another."

And so it went. Gallery after gallery, museum after museum, each response echoed the same sentiment – that Antonia was a minor artist, unworthy of recognition. After weeks of relentless pursuit and countless rejections, I slumped in my chair, feeling defeated.

"Is it really this hopeless?" I asked the empty room, tears prickling at the corners of my eyes.

I glanced over at one of Antonia's paintings, a hauntingly beautiful portrait of a woman with sorrowful eyes that seemed to look right through me. In that moment, I felt a surge of determination.

"Antonia would have kept going," I told myself, wiping away a tear. "She wouldn't have let these rejections stop her."

I took a deep breath and began drafting yet another email, my resolve rekindled by the memory of Antonia's unyielding spirit. This time, I would reach out to smaller galleries and alternative art spaces – perhaps they would see the true value in her work.

"Antonia," I whispered, "we'll find a way. I promise."

"Excuse me, Mr. Bellini?" I nervously held the phone to my ear, listening as Antonia's best friend hesitantly responded.

"Si, this is Giovanni Bellini. Who is calling?"

"Mr. Bellini, my name is Anthony Padgett. I'm an artist in England, and I've recently come across your friend's work... I was hoping to speak with you about her."

There was a long pause on the other end of the line, followed by a heavy sigh. "It has been many years since someone spoke of Antonia," he said, his voice thick with emotion. "What do you want to know?"

"Sir, I believe that Antonia's work is extraordinary, and I want to share it with the world," I declared, my passion evident in my voice. "But first, I need to restore some of her paintings and sculptures, which have suffered damage over the years. I also hope to learn more about her life and the inspirations behind her art."

"Antonia was a private person," Giovanni replied, his hesitation clear. "Her friends and family are not eager to expose her life to strangers."

"Please, Mr. Bellini," I implored, "I understand the sensitivity of the situation, but I promise that I only want to honor Antonia's memory and let her art touch people's lives. I assure you, I will handle her story with the utmost care and respect."

"Very well, Anthony" he conceded after a moment. "If you truly believe in my friend's talent, then you may visit my home in Italy. We can discuss this further."

"Thank you, Mr. Bellini – you won't regret this," I assured him, my heart pounding with anticipation.

"Perhaps," he said skeptically, before hanging up.

The weeks that followed were a whirlwind of activity. I secured a loan to finance the restoration of Antonia's art, knowing full well that it was a risk – one that could jeopardize my own future as an artist if I failed. Yet, as I painstakingly cleaned and repaired her masterpieces, I felt a deep connection to Antonia.

"Anthony," my friend Steph cautioned as she watched me work, "you're putting everything on the line for this woman. What if it doesn't pay off? Your career could be over before it even begins."

"Antonia's work deserves to be seen, Liz," I replied, my eyes never leaving the canvas. "I can't just walk away from her, knowing that her legacy might remain in obscurity forever."

With each stroke of my brush, I felt closer to Antonia, understanding her pain and joy through the layers of paint. I saw the world through her eyes – a world filled with beauty and darkness, love and despair. This connection fueled my determination to share her art with others, even if it meant risking everything I had worked so hard to achieve.

"Alright, Anthony," Steph said, clearly moved by my conviction. "If you're willing to take this chance, then I'll help you any way I can."

"Thank you, Steph" I smiled gratefully. "Together, we'll make sure that Antonia's name is remembered."

As we continued our work, I knew that the journey ahead would be fraught with challenges and heartache. But I also knew that, with each restored painting and sculpture, we were breathing new life into Antonia's story – a story that deserved to be told. And in the end, that was worth any price.

CHAPTER 15

The first time I saw Antonia Pageta's work, it was as if a secret door had been unlocked inside my soul. The vivid colors and swirling shapes spoke to me in ways no other art had before. As I stood there, a young art history student engulfed by the mesmerizing surrealist landscapes, I knew that this woman's talent deserved more recognition than it had ever received.

"Can you believe she was practically forgotten?" My professor whispered beside me, her voice tinged with disbelief. "A tragedy, isn't it?"

"A tragedy," I echoed, unable to tear my eyes away from the canvas. In that moment, I vowed to restore Antonia's legacy. It wasn't fair that someone so talented should be relegated to obscurity simply because the world hadn't been ready for her brilliance.

Antonia Pageta had been a force of nature – a beautiful, resilient artist ahead of her time. Her unwavering commitment to her artistic vision and her fierce independence were evident in every brushstroke. Born in a small village in Italy, Antonia had faced gender and racial biases that prevented her from enjoying the success she so richly deserved. But despite the challenges she faced, Antonia continued to create, her passionate spirit shining through each piece she produced.

"Anthony, you seem particularly drawn to Antonia's work," my professor observed, noticing the intensity of my gaze. "You know, I can see a bit of her spirit in you."

"Thank you, Professor," I replied, feeling a strange sense of kinship with this woman whose life had been so different from mine. "I just wish I could have met her."

"Ah, but you can still learn from her," my professor said with a knowing smile. "Her art speaks volumes about her life and experiences. If you listen closely enough, you'll hear her story."

As we walked through the rest of the exhibition, I couldn't help but feel a deep connection to Antonia. I wondered if she had ever felt as misunderstood and unappreciated as I sometimes did in my own life. And I knew that, like her, I would never let those feelings hold me back.

"Professor," I said with newfound determination, "I want to write my thesis on Antonia Pageta. I want the world to know her name and appreciate her art."

"An ambitious goal, Anthony," my professor replied, her eyes twinkling. "But I believe you have the passion and the drive to see it through. Let's get to work, shall we?"

"Absolutely." I smiled, feeling a rush of excitement at the prospect of bringing Antonia's story to light. It was a challenge I was more than ready to embrace.

I buried myself in research, visiting libraries and archives, pouring over Antonia's sketches, letters, and newspaper clippings. The more I learned about her life, the more I felt a connection to this remarkable woman. In one of her journals, I discovered Antonia's own words: "Art is my refuge from the world, but also my way of engaging with it."

Through my investigations, I managed to locate some people who had known Antonia personally. One elderly gentleman, Enzo, reminisced about how she would captivate everyone in the room with her stories and laughter, her eyes shining as brightly as her spirit.

"Antonia was like a storm," he said, his voice cracking with emotion. "She stirred everything up, leaving behind a path of beauty and destruction."

With each conversation, I felt even more inspired to share Antonia's work with the world. I began organizing a series of exhibitions, starting with a small gallery in a trendy neighborhood where contemporary art enthusiasts gathered.

"Welcome, everyone," I greeted visitors at the opening night, feeling both nervous and excited. "I hope you enjoy discovering Antonia Pageta's work as much as I did."

As the guests wandered around the gallery, I watched their reactions closely. Some appeared puzzled, while others seemed genuinely moved by the striking images before them.

"Powerful stuff, isn't it?" a woman commented, standing next to me as we admired one of Antonia's most provocative pieces. "I can't believe I've never heard of her before."

"Neither can I," I replied with a smile, seeing the first glimmers of recognition for Antonia's talent. "But that's what I'm here to change."

I spent months carefully curating each exhibition, selecting only the best works that represented Antonia's mastery of color, composition, and surreal imagery. As the shows gained traction and word spread, I was approached by larger galleries in different cities, eager to display her art.

"Antonia would have been so proud," Enzo told me one day as we stood in a bustling gallery filled with admirers of her work. "You've given her the recognition she always deserved."

"Thank you, Enzo," I responded, feeling a swell of pride and gratitude. "But this is just the beginning. I won't rest until Antonia's name is known far and wide."

And with that promise in my heart, I continued on my journey to restore Antonia's legacy, one exhibition at a time.

The ringing of my phone echoed through the small, cluttered office where I'd been spending countless hours researching Antonia's life. As I picked up the call, I recognized the crisp voice of a renowned museum curator, someone I had been trying to get in touch with for weeks.

"Mr. Padgett, I've reviewed the materials you sent, and I must say, Antonia Pageta's work is quite intriguing," she said, her tone cautious but curious.

"Thank you," I replied, elation bubbling inside me. "I truly believe her work deserves more recognition, and I'm sure an exhibition at your esteemed museum would be the perfect platform."

"Perhaps," she mused, pausing before continuing. "However, our schedule is booked solid for the next two years. I'll see if there's any room for flexibility, but I can't make any promises."

"Please do consider it," I urged, my heart pounding with anticipation. "Antonia's work has the power to inspire and challenge people, and I think it would be a tremendous loss if we let her contributions fade away."

"Alright, Mr. Padgett. I'll see what I can do," the curator promised, hanging up moments later. I knew this was only the first of many such calls I would have to make, but I was determined to give Antonia's legacy the attention it deserved.

As I continued reaching out to influential figures in the art world, I encountered resistance from conservative institutions who deemed Antonia's work too provocative or unconventional. Some critics dismissed her bold compositions as mere gimmicks, while others questioned the authenticity of her previously unknown works. These setbacks were disheartening, but I refused to let them deter me.

"Anthony, you need to understand that not everyone will appreciate Antonia's work," Enzo cautioned me one evening over dinner. "It's important to stay focused on the bigger picture."

"I know," I replied, picking at my food absentmindedly. "It's just frustrating to feel like I'm fighting an uphill battle against close-mindedness and prejudice."

"Keep pushing forward, Anthony," he encouraged me. "You have to do it for Antonia, and for all the other overlooked artists who deserve recognition."

As more obstacles arose, such as lack of funding for exhibitions and dealing with the harsh words of negative reviews, I found myself questioning whether my efforts would ever bear fruit. One evening, after reading a particularly scathing review, I sat alone in the dim light of my apartment.

"Is this all in vain?" I whispered into the silence, feeling the weight of discouragement press down on me. But then, as I glanced over at one of Antonia's paintings hanging on my wall, I felt a renewed sense of purpose.

"Her work matters," I reminded myself. And with that conviction, I continued to forge ahead, striving to ensure that Antonia Pageta's name would be remembered and celebrated in the annals of art history.

I knew I couldn't rely on traditional methods alone, so I started exploring alternative avenues to promote Antonia's work. Inspired by the resourcefulness of fellow art enthusiasts, I launched a crowdfunding campaign and shared it with my social media followers. The response was overwhelming – people from all corners of the globe came forward to support our cause, offering not only financial contributions but also their expertise and connections.

"Anthony, we received another generous donation," my friend Stephanie informed me one afternoon, her eyes gleaming with excitement as she checked the campaign's progress on her phone. "We're getting closer to our goal."

"Every little bit helps," I replied, my heart swelling with gratitude for the kindness of strangers who believed in Antonia's legacy as much as I did.

In addition to the crowdfunding campaign, I reached out to independent curators and organizations that championed underrepresented artists. Through these collaborations, new doors opened, providing us with opportunities to showcase Antonia's work in unconventional spaces.

"Anthony, I've secured a partnership with this fantastic underground gallery," my collaborator Claire announced during a video call. "The owner loves Antonia's work and wants to host an exhibition dedicated to her."

"Amazing!" I exclaimed, feeling a surge of hope that Antonia's art would finally reach the audience it deserved.

As each exhibition unfolded, I saw Antonia's work spark curiosity, surprise, and admiration in the eyes of visitors. They marveled at her innovative techniques, the vivid colors that seemed to dance on the canvas, and the profound themes that resonated through her art, transcending time and place.

"Her work is mesmerizing," a young woman whispered to her companion as they stood before one of Antonia's paintings, their faces bathed in the soft glow of the gallery lights. "I can't believe I've never heard of her before."

"Neither can I," her friend replied, shaking her head in disbelief. "She's a true genius."

As the art critics began to take notice, their reviews shifted from dismissive skepticism to genuine praise.

"Antonia Pageta's work is a revelation," wrote one critic in a prominent art magazine. "Her innovative approach to surrealism and her fearless exploration of deeply personal themes make her an artist of immense importance and relevance in today's world."

With each positive review and each exhibition that drew an ever-growing number of visitors, I could feel Antonia's legacy being restored, piece by piece. My heart soared with pride as I watched people from all walks of life connect with her art and recognize the invaluable contribution she had made to the world of creativity.

"Thank you, Anthony," Steph told me one evening after yet another successful opening night. "You've made Antonia's dream come true."

"Antonia deserves every bit of recognition," I responded softly, staring at the throngs of people still lingering in the gallery, discussing her work with fervor and admiration. "I'm just fortunate to be part of her story."

The gallery buzzed with excitement as people gathered around the works of Antonia Pageta, their faces reflecting a mix of awe and curiosity. My heart raced as I spotted the director of a prominent museum standing by one of Antonia's boldest paintings, her eyes wide with admiration.

"Mr. Padgett, it's an honor to meet you," she said, extending her hand. "I'm Victoria Marquez, the director of the National Museum of Modern Art."

"Likewise, Ms. Marquez," I replied, shaking her hand firmly. The weight of her presence filled the room.

"Your dedication to bringing Antonia Pageta's work back into the spotlight is commendable," she continued. "Her pieces are extraordinary, and I would be honored to acquire some of them for our permanent collection."

"Antonia's work speaks for itself," I said, my voice full of pride. "It's been a privilege to share her art with others."

"Mr. Padgett, I was hoping you could join me in discussing your efforts at an upcoming conference on underrepresented artists," she added. "Your story is inspiring, and it would be a valuable addition to our event."

"Of course! It would be an honor." I felt a surge of accomplishment at the invitation, knowing that my determination to restore Antonia's legacy had not gone unnoticed.

A renowned art historian, Dr. Jameson, approached us, his eyes sparkling with enthusiasm as he held a copy of his latest book. "Anthony, I've been following your work, and I wanted you to have the first copy of my new publication," he said, handing it to me. "It's about Antonia Pageta's life and her impact on the art world. Your efforts inspired me to delve deeper into her story."

"Thank you, Dr. Jameson." I clutched the book, feeling the weight of Antonia's legacy in my hands. "I can't wait to read it."

"Anthony Padgett?" A journalist from a major art publication approached me, extending her hand. "My editor has been raving about the exhibitions you've organized. We'd love to interview you and discuss your journey in restoring Antonia Pageta's legacy."

"Absolutely," I replied, my cheeks flushed with pride. "I'd be happy to share our story with your readers."

As the night wore on, I mingled with the influential figures who had gathered to celebrate Antonia's work. Their words of support and encouragement left me feeling invigorated and filled with purpose.

As I gazed upon Antonia's paintings, I could almost hear her whispering in my ear, urging me to continue fighting for her place in history. And with each accolade, each kind word, and each new opportunity, I knew that I was one step closer to ensuring that her legacy would never be forgotten.

Months had passed since the first exhibition, and I watched in awe as Antonia's work continued to gain momentum. It was a bright summer afternoon, and I stood at the entrance of yet another gallery filled with her paintings. The sun's rays filtered through the large windows, casting a warm glow on the vibrant colors and bold strokes that adorned the canvas.

"Anthony, it's incredible how far you've come in bringing Antonia's work to the forefront," my dear friend and fellow curator, Elena, said as she took my arm. "These exhibitions have truly transformed the way people view her art."

"Thank you, Elena," I replied, my heart swelling with pride. "I couldn't have done it without your support and guidance."

The gallery buzzed with excitement, as visitors meandered through the space, engaging in hushed conversations about the significance of Antonia's art. I overheard a group of educators discussing plans to incorporate her work into their curriculum, exposing a new generation to the genius of Antonia Pageta.

"Mr. Padgett?" A young woman approached me, clutching a copy of the book written by Dr. Jameson. "I just wanted to say thank you for all you've done to bring Antonia's work to light. As an aspiring artist myself, her story has been truly inspiring."

"Thank you," I said, touched by her words. "Antonia's talent deserves to be recognized, and I'm honored to play a part in that."

"Excuse me, Anthony?" A voice called out from behind me. I turned to see a middle-aged man, his face a mix of both curiosity and admiration. "I represent an organization that funds educational programs in the arts. We're interested in developing a scholarship in Antonia's name, dedicated to supporting underrepresented artists. Could we discuss this further?"

"Of course," I replied, feeling a surge of excitement. "I'd love to be involved in such a project."

As the final visitors trickled out of the gallery, I took a moment to pause and reflect on the journey that had led me here. Antonia's work was finally receiving the recognition it deserved, and her legacy was being restored for future generations to appreciate.

I thought about the countless hours spent researching her life, organizing exhibitions, and advocating for her place in art history. It hadn't been easy, but the impact of my efforts was now clear. In the quiet solitude of the empty gallery, I felt a deep sense of accomplishment and fulfillment.

"Antonia," I whispered, my voice echoing through the room. "Your art will live on, and your story will inspire countless others who have been overlooked and undervalued."

As I walked out of the gallery, I felt a renewed sense of purpose. My work to promote underrepresented artists like Antonia was far from over, but I knew that each step I took would bring their voices closer to the spotlight they so rightfully deserved.

CHAPTER 16

The sun dipped below the horizon, casting a warm glow over the museum's high ceilings and polished marble floors. The last rays of light danced on the walls, intermingling with the shadows cast by the breathtaking works that adorned them. A hushed reverence filled the air, as if even the echoes of shuffling footsteps and hushed whispers were afraid to disturb the sanctity of the space. In my chest, a dull ache twisted like a knot, reminding me of the loss of Antonia, yet simultaneously filling me with pride at her legacy.

"Antonia Pageta passed away some years ago," I said, my voice barely above a whisper, "but her influence on the art world continues to grow stronger with each passing day."

My words hung in the air, absorbed by the silence that dominated the gallery. It was almost as if her spirit lingered here, watching over her masterpieces, guiding the hands of those who would carry her artistic torch into the future. Antonia had defied convention and expectation, forging a path in the art world that had been deemed impossible for one from such humble beginnings. She had shattered barriers, proving that talent and perseverance could triumph even in the face of adversity.

"Her work is revolutionary," I continued, emotions swelling within me. "Each piece is a testament to her incredible vision, her unwavering commitment to pushing boundaries and challenging norms."

As we moved through the gallery, I could see the impact Antonia's artwork had on those who beheld it. Their eyes widened, their breaths caught, and for a moment, they were transported to another realm, a place where the lines between reality and imagination blurred and intertwined. Her surrealist landscapes captivated and inspired, igniting something deep within the souls of those who allowed themselves to truly see.

"Antonia may be gone," I concluded, my voice heavy with emotion, "but her art lives on, touching countless lives and forever altering the landscape of the art world."

"Motherhood" was Antonia's most famous piece, a stunning portrayal of the bond between a mother and child. The canvas seemed to breathe with life, the colors blending organically to create an image that defied logic yet resonated deeply within the viewer. It had been celebrated by critics and adored by art-lovers alike, securing its place in the annals of art history.

"Her ability to capture the essence of human emotion is unparalleled," I said to the group of visitors gathered around me in the gallery. "Antonia Pageta's work transcends any specific time or place — it speaks to the very core of our shared humanity."

My name is Anthony Padgett, and when I discovered Antonia's secret studio, I knew that I had stumbled upon something extraordinary. From that moment on, I dedicated myself to preserving her legacy and ensuring that her name would not be forgotten.

"Did you know her personally?" a woman in the group asked, her eyes taking in the striking details of the painting before us.

"Unfortunately, I never had the chance to meet Antonia," I replied softly, my words tinged with sadness. "By the time I found her work, she had already passed away. But through studying her art and piecing together the fragments of her story, I feel as if I've come to know her intimately."

My journey into Antonia's world had been one of tireless research and emotional investment. As I followed the trail of her life, I became more and more connected to the woman who had created these masterpieces. Her determination and resilience in the face of adversity spoke to me in a way that no other artist ever had.

"See how she plays with light and shadow in 'The Labyrinth'?" I gestured towards another captivating piece, where figures moved through a maze-like landscape, their faces obscured by the darkness. "She was a true visionary, unafraid to delve into the deepest recesses of the human psyche."

"Her art is a reflection of her own soul," I continued, my voice filled with admiration. "She poured herself into each and every piece, leaving behind a treasure trove of emotion and beauty for us to explore."

As I led the group through the gallery, I couldn't help but feel a sense of pride in all that I had accomplished. Antonia's story had become my life's work, and I was determined to share it with the world. It was as if I could feel her spirit beside me, guiding me along this path and whispering her gratitude for my unwavering dedication. And in that moment, I knew that Antonia Pageta's legacy would live on – forever immortalized in the hearts and minds of those who were fortunate enough to experience her extraordinary art.

I had spent countless hours researching Antonia's life, piecing together her story from old letters, journal entries, and interviews with those who had known her. I was determined to ensure that Antonia's legacy would not be forgotten, and so I gathered all the information I could find and began writing a comprehensive biography.

"Antonia Pageta: A Life in Art" became my magnum opus; an exhaustive account of her life and work, filled with stunning photographs of her paintings, sketches, and sculptures. I made it my mission to share Antonia's story with as many people as possible, organizing lectures at universities and art institutes across the country.

"Thank you all for coming," I said, standing at the podium in front of a packed auditorium. "Today, I want to introduce you to the incredible world of Antonia Pageta, a woman whose art has been lost to history for far too long."

As I spoke, I could see the audience's interest piqued, their eyes widening in awe as I unveiled each breathtaking piece on the projector screen. I could feel Antonia's spirit watching over me, urging me on as I passionately advocated for her rightful place in art history.

"Anthony, thank you for your presentation," said Professor Anderson, a renowned art historian. "Your dedication to preserving Antonia's legacy is truly inspiring."

"Thank you," I replied, feeling a surge of pride. "It's an honor to bring her story back to life."

"Anthony, your book has opened our eyes to Antonia's genius," another guest chimed in. "We've decided to add her work to our permanent collection at the museum."

"Really?" I asked, tears prickling at the corners of my eyes. "This means so much to me, and I know it would have meant the world to her."

"Her art deserves recognition," the curator said, nodding solemnly.

As word spread about Antonia's work and her extraordinary story, the art world began to take notice. Exhibitions were held in major cities across Europe and the United States; articles were published in prestigious art magazines, and her pieces sold for astronomical sums at auction houses worldwide.

Antonia's legacy had been reborn, and I knew that my tireless efforts had played a part in that. The woman who had once been forgotten was now celebrated as one of the greatest surrealist artists of her time, her name etched into the annals of art history forevermore.

"Thank you, Antonia," I whispered, standing alone amidst her paintings at a gallery opening. "I hope I've done you proud."

And as the soft murmurs of impressed visitors washed over me, I couldn't help but think that somewhere out there, Antonia Pageta was smiling down upon us all.

The steady stream of accolades and recognition for Antonia's artwork seemed to be never-ending. Just last week, she had been posthumously awarded the prestigious Golden Brush Award, a high honor in the art world. As I held the gleaming trophy in my hands, a wave of pride washed over me. Antonia deserved every bit of this recognition.

"Anthony, this is an incredible achievement," said Stephanie, an art critic and friend who had been one of the first to advocate for Antonia's work. "Antonia's paintings are finally getting the attention they deserve."

"Thank you, Steph," I replied, clutching the award tightly. "I've always known her artwork was extraordinary, and now the world knows it too."

What set Antonia's art apart was her unique approach to Surrealism. Her paintings were like windows into otherworldly realms, blending fantastical elements with subtle nods to reality. The way she played with light and shadow, creating a sense of depth that drew the viewer in, was unparalleled. She had an uncanny ability to evoke emotions through her brushstrokes, with each piece speaking volumes about the human experience.

"Have you seen 'The Dreamer's Labyrinth'?" Steph asked, pointing to one of Antonia's most famous works. "It's as if she's inviting us to explore our deepest fears and desires."

I nodded, recalling the countless hours Antonia had spent on that particular painting. "She told me it represented the maze of the human mind, with its twists and turns symbolizing the complexity of our thoughts and emotions."

"Remarkable," Steph murmured, her eyes locked on the painting. "No wonder her work is so highly sought after. It's not just visually stunning, but also profoundly thought-provoking."

As we continued to admire Antonia's art, I couldn't help but reflect on how far we had come. From the days when her paintings were hidden away in a dusty attic, to now gracing the walls of prestigious galleries and museums worldwide – it was nothing short of a miracle.

"Antonia's work has truly left an indelible mark on the art world," Steph said, echoing my thoughts. "And you, Anthony, have played such an important role in sharing her story and preserving her legacy."

I smiled softly, feeling a sense of fulfillment I could never have imagined. My mission to bring Antonia's genius to light had been a long, arduous journey, but every step had been worth it. As people continued to discover and appreciate her artwork, I knew that Antonia's spirit would live on through her breathtaking creations.

"Thank you, Steph," I replied, my heart swelling with pride. "I couldn't have done it without your support, and the support of so many others who believed in Antonia's talent. Her art has touched countless lives, and I feel honored to have played a part in sharing her incredible gifts with the world."

The hushed whispers of museum visitors filled the spacious gallery, creating a hum that buzzed in my ears. I stood before one of Antonia's most powerful works, "The Bridge Between Worlds" - an enigmatic piece depicting a woman standing on the edge of a precipice, reaching out to grasp the hand of a mysterious figure shrouded in mist.

"Antonia's paintings evoke such strong emotions," remarked a young woman to her companion as they gazed at the piece. "You can almost feel the desperation and hope in the woman's expression."

"Absolutely," agreed her friend. "It's like a window into her soul, revealing her deepest fears and desires."

I couldn't help but smile at their words, knowing Antonia would have been thrilled by the impact her work was having on viewers. She had poured her heart and soul into her art, and it was evident in every brushstroke.

"Anthony," Steph whispered, leaning closer to me. "Look at that couple over there. They seem completely captivated by 'The Dreamer's Lament.'"

I glanced across the room to see a man and woman, their eyes brimming with tears, as they studied the hauntingly beautiful scene of a lone figure weeping beneath a moonlit sky. It was as if Antonia's work had reached out and touched something deep within them, stirring memories and emotions long buried.

"Her art has the power to move people," I thought to myself, feeling a surge of pride. "Even after her passing, Antonia continues to inspire and challenge us through her incredible creations."

"Her work transcends the boundaries of time and space," Steph continued, her voice filled with awe. "It speaks to the very core of our human experience."

As we wandered through the exhibit, I felt the weight of Antonia's presence all around us. The air seemed charged with the energy of her spirit, the walls echoing with the sounds of her laughter and the whispers of her dreams. It was as if she had infused every piece with a part of herself, leaving an indelible mark on each canvas.

"Antonia's art has the power to heal," I murmured, lost in thought. "It has brought people together from all walks of life, united by a shared sense of wonder and appreciation."

"Indeed," Steph nodded. "Her work is a testament to the depth of her talent and the strength of her vision."

As I stood before one final painting, "The Eternal Dance" - a vibrant, swirling kaleidoscope of color and movement - I felt a sudden wave of emotion wash over me. Tears filled my eyes as I realized that, through her artwork, Antonia's legacy would continue to live on, touching the hearts and minds of countless individuals for generations to come.

"Thank you, Antonia," I whispered, my voice barely audible. "For sharing your gift with the world, and for allowing me the privilege of helping to preserve your extraordinary story."

As the museum doors closed behind us, I couldn't help but feel a deep sense of satisfaction. I knew that Antonia and I had accomplished something remarkable together, even if she wasn't there to see it unfold.

"Anthony," Steph said, her eyes glistening with emotion, "You've given Antonia the recognition she deserves. Thank you for your dedication."

"Thank you, Steph," I replied, feeling humbled by her gratitude. "It's been an honor to play a part in sharing Antonia's work with the world."

We stepped outside into the crisp autumn air, watching as leaves danced through the streets, mimicking the movement of Antonia's brush strokes. The city seemed more alive than ever, pulsing with the energy of creativity and inspiration.

"Her influence is everywhere," I thought, smiling to myself. "Antonia's spirit has ignited something within all of us."

"Hey, Anthony!" A fellow artist called out, waving from across the street. "I just saw the exhibit! Antonia's paintings are incredible!"

"Thank you!" I shouted back, my heart swelling with pride. "Spread the word; let everyone know about Antonia Pageta!"

As I walked away, with Steph, I pondered the lasting impact that Antonia's art would have on generations to come. Her fearless exploration of the human experience, her unwavering commitment to her vision, and her undeniable talent were now etched into the annals of art history, forever changing the landscape.

"Antonia may be gone," I whispered to myself, "but her spirit will live on through her art and the countless lives it touches."

With every step I took, I felt the warmth of Antonia's presence beside me – a guiding force, encouraging me to continue fighting for what I believed in. As the sun dipped below the horizon, casting its final rays upon the city, I knew that, together, Antonia and I had changed the world.